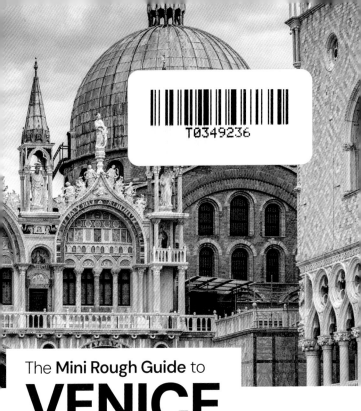

The **Mini Rough Guide** to
VENICE

ROUGH
GUIDES

YOUR TAILOR-MADE TRIP
STARTS HERE

Tailor-made trips and unique adventures crafted by local experts

HOW ROUGHGUIDES.COM/TRIPS WORKS

STEP 1

Pick your dream destination, tell us what you want and submit an enquiry.

STEP 2

Fill in a short form to tell your local expert about your dream trip and preferences.

STEP 3

Our local expert will craft your tailor-made itinerary. You'll be able to tweak and refine it until you're completely satisfied.

STEP 4

Book online with ease, pack your bags and enjoy the trip! Our local expert will be on hand 24/7 while you're on the road.

PLAN AND BOOK YOUR TRIP AT
ROUGHGUIDES.COM/TRIPS

How to download your Free eBook

1. Visit **www.roughguides.com/ free-ebook** or scan the **QR code** opposite

2. Enter the code **venice795**

3. Follow the simple step-by-step instructions

For troubleshooting contact: mail@roughguides.com

Contents

Introduction

Venice is the place we have all been to, if only in our imagination. For an unbroken 1,100 years *La Serenissima*, the Serene Republic, was an independent empire, with a constitution that is studied to this day. In the 9th century, while most European cities were hidden behind defensive walls, Venice stood open to the world, protected only by its lagoon. As a tantalising blend of East and West, Venice was neither totally European nor wholly Italian. Byzantine domes, Eastern mosaics and Gothic palaces still evoke this exotic legacy, even if the city enchants us as much for its timelessness and aloofness from modern life.

But contemporary Venice is being bold again, with a sleek bridge over the Grand Canal, a mobile flood barrier nearly completed, designer bed and breakfasts, stylish wine bars, and a cutting-edge contemporary art museum facing St Mark's. It's a

WHAT'3 NEW

After decades of delays and scandals and a collective holding of breath during a flood in 2020, the city exhaled with measured relief when its long-awaited MOSE (flood barrier) apparatus passed its first real-life test, protecting the city for the first time from high tides (*acque alte*). The massive mechanism has been activated around 20 times in each of the ensuing years (far more than expected), and while Venice certainly remains in peril, Venetians are grateful at least that their priceless heritage has been kept largely dry. In the meantime, restoration works have moved along at pace: the gorgeous central apse of Torcello's magnificent ancient cathedral has regained its shine, as has Canova's striking cenotaph in the Frari Church and the famous Accademia Bridge. Not least, ample progress has been made on the restructuring of the city's most famous depository of arts, the Gallerie dell'Accademia, currently displaying its largest ever array of invaluable works of Venetian art.

delicate balancing act: visitors also come for the gondolas, the Gothic architecture and the sense of being marooned in a gorgeous Disneyland for grown-ups.

GEOGRAPHY

The sea has always been linked with the city's fortunes and, like the swampy, shallow Venetian lagoon, it is both loved and feared. Situated at the northwestern end of the Adriatic Sea, Venice lies on an archipelago in a crescent-shaped lagoon 50km (32 miles) in length. Greater Venice stands on 118 flat islets, with its buildings supported by millions of larch poles driven into sediment. Crisscrossing the city is a labyrinth of over 160 canals, spanned by more than 400 bridges. These canals are partly flushed out by the tides that sweep in daily from the Adriatic through three channels that pierce the ring of sand bars *(lidi)* protecting the lagoon. However, given the rising sea levels, Venice has been increasingly swept by sporadic winter floods, hence the demand for a tidal barrier. But environmentalists believe that Venice's problems are a microcosm of those affecting many other cities and that it's not too late to save Venice and the Venetians.

Decorative Venetian mask

NAVIGATING THE CITY

Any visitor to Venice has to confront its unique

geography. Exploring the city properly means pounding the canal-sides and clambering the many bridges. Travel light and leap on a *vaporetto* (waterbus) when flagging. The ferries ply the Grand Canal, but will also whisk you out to the islands of the Venetian lagoon – from the Lido beaches to the brightly painted houses on Burano, or from Murano's glass showrooms to Torcello's medieval cathedral, set amid remote salt marshes. You can even inspect the controversial mobile flood barrier, which should be fully functioning by 2025. Yet even if the physical threats come from the sea, the social challenges are no less serious. Venice may be mired in its glorious past, with Gothic palaces galore, but it needs to retain its population if it is to stave off its fate as a theme park.

MEET THE VENETIANS

Since the population fell below 50,000 in 2022, the city has had a rude wake-up call. In its heyday, the city of Venice had 200,000 inhabitants – a figure that fell to 90,000 at the end of the Republic

---

SUSTAINABLE TRAVEL

Tourism has become both the lifeblood and the bane of Venice, with almost six million tourists visiting in 2023. Efforts to confront overtourism have included a ban on cruise ships in 2021 and the introduction of a day-tripper fee in 2024. Calls for more sustainable tourism are increasingly backed by investment in culture and crafts. You can now learn to cook with a Venetian countess or embark on a craft course with Cannaregio artisans. If you're feeling daring, try kayaking or row standing up, gondolier-style.

Your gift to ordinary Venetians is not simply to daydream your way through the city but to drift a while with them, and to support local culture. Lose yourself in the backwaters and mingle with the Venetians themselves. Whether it's staying in a bed and breakfast, attending a Baroque recital, or seeking out traditional crafts, you are helping Venice survive.

WHEN TO GO

Venice's tourist season is very nearly an all-year affair. If you can, aim to visit in May or October – the crowds in April and from June to September can be frustrating, the heat uncomfortable (though not as stifling as on the mainland), and hotel prices high. While the city can be dank and cold in winter, it takes on a rather mystical beauty at this time. Christmas and New Year in Venice have also become fashionable times to visit. During these and other major holidays and festival periods (notably late winter's Carnival and Easter week), hotel prices are at their highest and advance reservations essential. Note that *acqua alta*, Venice's seasonal flooding, is far more frequent than it used to be: between October and late February, it's not uncommon for flooding to occur for several days in succession.

Gondolier on a break

and currently stands at around 49,000. Venice's resident population keeps shrinking, leaving the Venetians an endangered species. Whether craftsmen or boat builders, the locals are struggling to survive in a city dedicated to other people's dreams. Architect Francesco da Mosto worries whether his children will be the last generation to go to school in Venice. Chef Enrica Rocca mocks her neighbourhood as a place in which 'you can buy a mask more easily than milk'.

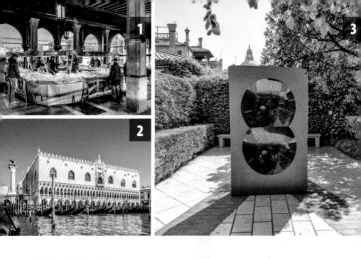

10 Things not to miss

A perfect day in Venice

9.00AM

Morning market. Feast your eyes on the fish, fruit and vegetables of the Rialto markets, where stalls have been in business for over 1,000 years.

10.00AM

Grand Canal. From the Rialto take *vaporetto* No. 1 in the San Marco/Lido direction. Observe the locals going about their morning routines. Glide past the parade of palaces and alight at Accademia.

11.00AM

Gallery visit. You're now in the *sestiere* of Dorsoduro, a haven for art lovers. Explore the Accademia, housing the world's greatest collection of Venetian art, before watching the mesmerising water traffic on the Accademia Bridge.

1.00PM

Lunch with a view. Take your pick from the open-air cafés and restaurants on the Zattere, the panoramic quayside skirting the southern side of the Dorsoduro. Try Gelateria Nico (see page 119), one of the best ice cream parlours in town.

2.00PM

Gentle stroll. Stretch your legs along the Zattere, popping into the Gesuati church to check out the Tiepolo ceiling. Head to the tip of the peninsula where the Punta della Dogana

has been transformed into a cutting-edge contemporary art gallery, then go admire the monumental La Salute Basilica.

3.00PM

Bellini time. Hop on a *vaporetto* to Vallaresso landing stage across the Grand Canal. Pass Harry's Bar (see page 117) and head north to Salizzada San Moisé and Calle Larga XXII Marzo to browse some of the smartest shops in town.

4.00PM

Tea break. In Piazza San Marco, splash out on tea at Caffè Florian (see page 117), the walls of its lavish rooms adorned with doges, artisans and other distinguished Venetians. Next, wander along the Riva degli Schiavoni quayside.

6.30PM

Drink with the locals. Explore the streets and squares of the Castello region behind the Riva, admiring the abundance of graceful, arched windows.

8.00PM

Dinner on the Zattere. Enjoy a romantic evening in Lineadombra (see page 119) a simple, elegant design-conscious restaurant.

10.00PM

Rooftop drinks. Cross the Giudecca Canal by *vaporetto* to Skyline (see page 123), a cool rooftop haunt in the Hilton Molino Stucky.

Exploring the lagoon

7.00AM

Morning coffee. Start the day with an
espresso before boarding the #12 *vaporetto*
(waterbus) from Fondamente Nove. If weather
obliges, you'll enjoy distant views of the Alps
as you glide past San Michele and Murano,
alighting on Burano after a 40-minute ride.

8.20AM

Stroll 'n' snap. Wander Burano's colourful
canalside streets, lined with pastel-hued
homes. It's a photographer's dream.

9.45AM

Island hopping. Board the *vaporetti* #9 (every
15min) for the 5-minute ride to tiny Torcello.
This marshy, unprepossessing spot was the
site of the original settlement in the Venetian
lagoon.

10.15AM

A spot of culture. Explore the magnificent
Basilica di Santa Maria Assunta, the oldest
church in the entire lagoon. It's adorned with
some of the finest ancient mosaics in Italy.
On the same square, peek into the simpler,
Romanesque Church of Santa Fosca and the
Museo di Torcello.

12.00PM

Lunch. On your return walk, take a rest near
the ancient Ponte del Diavolo to lunch at the
restaurant of the same name (see page 123).

Get the catch of the day, enjoyed in its peaceful
garden, before catching the #9 back to Burano.

1.30PM

Head to a museum. As well as for its looks,
Burano is famous for its lace and linen. Take the
10-minute stroll through town to visit the small
Museo del Merletto (Lace Museum).

2.20PM

Mooch around Murano. Catch the #12 to
reach Murano, "Mini Venice," a 30-minute ride.
Like Venice, its islands are divided by canals
and lined with mansions and palazzi. It even
has its own Grand Canal. But Murano's *raison
d'être* has always been the making of glass. To
observe this artform, exclusively reserved for
the Muranese since 1291, head to the Murano
Glass Museum, then watch masters at work in
the deconsecrated Glass Cathedral.

4.00PM

Byzantine beauty. There's an hour left before
Murano's magnificent Basilica of Santa Maria
e San Donato closes. Like Torcello's illustrious
church, Murano's too boasts 7th-century
foundations.

5.00PM

Views and vino. Cap off your tour where it
began: at the Fondamente Nove. Steps away is
Algiubagio (see page 121), a modern *bacaro*
with wonderful views over the lagoon.

Historical Venice

9AM

Venetian masterpieces. Begin around the corner from Piazza San Marco at the Gothic-style Doge's Palace. The heart of Venetian political life for centuries, its lavish chambers reflect the emergence of Venetian power. Here, you'll admire works of local masters like Tintoretto, Veronese and Titian.

10AM

Soak up some history. Rather than entering Saint Mark's, head east along the awakening Riva past the Bridge of Sighs to the Church of San Zaccaria. Since the early 9th century, it has sheltered the relics of the father of John the Baptist. Don't miss the watery crypt, resting place of early doges.

11AM

An architectural gem. Circle back toward Piazza San Marco via the Ponte de Canonica. It's time to enter the city's most storied basilica, decked with 8,000 square metres of glittering mosaics. Like the Doge's Palace, the treasures of Saint Mark's bear out *La Serenissima's* rising eminence and power, housing Venice's patron saint (smuggled from Alexandria in the 9th century) and the sublime four Horses of Saint Mark (stolen from Constantinople in 1204).

1.30PM

Museums. Once you've rested your legs in a grand café on the square or a *bacaro* in the alleys just beyond, climb the stairs from Piazza San Marco's west end for the broadest survey of Venetian history on offer: linked together are the Museo Correr, Museo Archeologico and Biblioteca Marciana, housing classical statuary, 15th-century globes and works by Veronese and Tintoretto.

2.30PM

Afternoon stroll. Wind through the *calli* to the north, crossing the Campo Santa Maria Formosa en route to the imposing Basilica dei Santi Giovanni e Paolo – "Venice's Pantheon," so-called for the long list of doges buried in the vast interior.

3.00PM

Coffee and culture. A short hop away is a colourful marble masterpiece: The Chiesa di Santa Maria dei Miracoli, its late 15th-century completion trumpeting the arrival of the Renaissance in Venice. After stepping inside, savour the view of the church over the canal with a coffee and *cannolo* in the charming Campo Santa Maria Nova.

4.00PM

Wander through the market. Make a leisurely crossing of the Rialto Bridge to wind through the Rialto market, one of Europe's financial hubs for centuries, packed with produce stalls, shops and enchantingly stylish *bacari* (tapas bars), the perfect end to a day of exploring.

History

It may be hard to believe, but this tiny city was once the centre of the wealthiest, most powerful state in Europe. In its prime, Venice influenced the course of modern history, leaving an incomparable legacy in the shape of the city itself.

EARLY VENETIANS

Although the earliest Venetians were fishermen and boatmen skilled at navigating the shallow lagoon's islands, the first major settlers arrived after the Lombards invaded in AD 568. The invasion led the coastal dwellers to flee to low-lying offshore islands in the lagoon, such as Torcello and Malamocco, on the string of *lidi*, or barrier beaches, on the Adriatic.

Venetia, or Venezia, was the name of the entire area at the northern end of the Adriatic under the Roman Empire. Venice as we know it developed gradually around a cluster of small islands that remained out of reach of the north Italian Lombard kingdom and were subject only to lose control from the Roman-Byzantine centre at Ravenna, which answered to Constantinople. Around AD 697 the lagoon communities were united under a separate military command, set up at Malamocco, with a *dux* (Latin for leader), or doge, in charge, though subordinate to the Byzantine emperor.

---- NOTES ----

When St Mark's relics reached Venice c.829, a chapel (the original St Mark's) was built for them next to the Palazzo Ducale. Mark's winged lion emblem was adopted as the symbol of the city.

The Lombards were succeeded on the mainland in 774 by Charlemagne's Frankish army, and in 810 his son Pépin was sent to conquer the communities of the lagoon. Pépin seized the outer island of Malamocco, but the doge and his entourage managed to escape to the safety of the Rivo Alto (High Shore), the future Rialto, where they built a fortress on the site now housing the Palazzo Ducale (Doge's Palace).

THE RISE OF THE REPUBLIC

The new city gradually became independent of distant Byzantium, prospering due to tight control of the north Italian river deltas and, later, of the sea itself. Fishing, salt and the lumber and slave trades enriched the city, and rival producers and traders were ruthlessly quashed. From the 9th century, in defiance of the pope and the Byzantine emperor, the Venetians traded with the Islamic world, selling luxuries from Constantinople at a high profit to the rest of Europe. By this time, Venice was no longer a dependency of the Byzantine Empire, and, to underline this, snatched the body of St

St Mark's trademark lion

Mark from Muslim-controlled Alexandria, in Egypt, c.829. Mark replaced the Byzantine saint, Theodore, as the patron of Venice.

EMPIRE BUILDING

The city's newly founded Arsenale turned out fleets of ever-mightier galleys, enabling Venice to move into the Adriatic, where it warred for decades with its bitter enemy, the Dalmatia. In the year 1000, the Republic scored a significant victory and celebrated it with a 'marriage to the sea' ceremony, which is still re-enacted annually (see page 105). Ships flying St Mark's pennant ranged over the Aegean Sea and the eastern Mediterranean, trading, plundering and bringing back spoils to strengthen the state. Venice soon came to be known as the *Serenissima* (Most Serene Republic), or 'Queen of the Seas'.

From the start of the Crusades in 1095, the Venetians sensed rich pickings. Ideally positioned both politically and geographically between Europe and the East, and with little concern for the spiritual aspect of the campaigns, Venice produced and outfitted ships and equipped knights, often at huge profit.

Crusader armies sacked Constantinople, the greatest repository of the ancient world's treasures, under the 90-year-old Doge Enrico Dandalo in 1204. Among the rich pickings were the four bronze horses that adorn the Basilica di San Marco.

At the end of the 13th century, the Venetians curbed the power of the doges, evolving into a patrician oligarchy. Eventually, the doges

MARCO POLO

Venice's most famous citizen opened the eyes of 13th-century Europe to the irresistibly exotic mysteries of East Asia. While recent scholarship has thrown some doubt on the authenticity of his story, Marco Polo relates how, for some 20 years, he served the Mongol Emperor Kublai Khan and was the first Westerner permitted to travel about freely in China.

Battle of Lepanto 1571

became little more than pampered prisoners in their palace, stripped of every vestige of authority; their primary function was to preside over the Republic's pompous festivities, and after 1310 no major change was made in the constitution until the Republic fell in 1797.

WARS AND INTRIGUE

Venice spent much of the 14th century battling with its rival, Genoa, over the slave and grain trades in the Black Sea. They also fought over the route from the Mediterranean north to Bruges and Antwerp, where spices and other wares could be traded for prized Flemish cloth, English wool and tin. In 1379, during the fourth and final Genoese War, Venice only narrowly avoided absolute defeat, having lost the key port of Chioggia. The port was recovered, however, and in 1380 Genoa surrendered, forever finished as a major maritime force.

Doge Loredan

The 14th century was also a time for domestic difficulties. In 1310 a group of disgruntled aristocrats under Baiamonte Tiepolo tried to seize power and kill the doge, but their revolt was quickly crushed. Worse was to come: between 1347 and 1349 almost half of the city's population of 120,000 was wiped out by the Black Death. A further 20,000 Venetians died in another epidemic in 1382, and over the next three centuries the city was almost never free of plague.

In the 15th century, Venice's expanding borders to the west helped spark the Lombard Wars (1423–1454). The Republic defended its new territory so tenaciously that Milan, Florence and Naples formed an anti-Venice coalition, worried that Venice might take over the entire Italian peninsula.

NEW THREATS IN A GOLDEN AGE

With the dying Byzantine Empire no longer able to buffer Venice against threats from the east, a new rival arose in the shape of the Ottoman Empire. Initially, the young sultan, Mohammed the Conqueror, was not taken seriously, and inadequate forces were sent by the Venetians to protect Constantinople. In 1453 the city fell to the Turks, who played havoc with Venetian trade routes and won a key naval battle at Negroponte in the northern Aegean in

1470. Although Venice was still the leading Mediterranean maritime power, these defeats marked the beginning of a downhill slide.

While its fortunes beyond the lagoon waned, Venetian civilisation reached new heights. No building in the Western world was more sumptuous than the Palazzo Ducale; no church had as many treasures as San Marco. And as artists such as Bellini, Giorgione, Carpaccio, Tintoretto, Veronese and Titian flourished, Andrea Palladio's revolutionary concepts began to shape the future of architecture. Venice was also home to the most complex economy and the richest culture in all of Europe.

Yet the threats to the Republic continued to accumulate. The revolutionary new trade routes launched by Vasco da Gama and Christopher Columbus ended Venice's spice-trade monopoly. The axis of power in Europe gradually moved to countries on the Atlantic coast. As trade with the New World mushroomed, trade with Asia that had long ensured Venetian prosperity fell into decline.

DECLINE AND DECADENCE

After the French invasion of Italy in 1494, Venice sought to further encroach on Northern Italian territories. However, this international brinkmanship so incensed the rest of Europe that, in 1508, under the auspices of Pope Julius II and the king of Spain, a pan-European organisation, known as the League of Cambrai, was formed with the aim of destroying the Republic. Though nearly succeeding, the League itself fell apart through internal struggles, sparing Venice. Eight years of war, however, had cost the Venetians dearly, putting a stop to their ambitions in Italy. Furthermore, with Charles V's Empire steadily accumulating Italian ground, considerable Venetian diplomacy was needed for the city to preserve its independence.

Around the eastern and southern Mediterranean, the Ottomans surged on, but the Battle of Lepanto, in 1571, finally turned the Turkish tide. The fleet of the Holy League was spearheaded by Venice, but the allies, by now suspicious of Venice, ensured that the

View of the Ducal Palace in Venice (c.1755) by Canaletto

city did not profit from this victory; instead of continuing the offensive east, they signed away the Venetian stronghold of Cyprus as part of the peace treaty.

From 1575 to 1577 plague raged again, and the population fell from 150,000 to 100,000. Despite this, and the Republic's diminishing political powers, Venice prospered through the 16th and 17th centuries, aided by the skills and contacts of Jewish refugees from the Italian peninsula and Spain. Music flourished, with Claudio Monteverdi in the 17th century and Antonio Vivaldi in the 18th. Venice's art tradition continued with Tiepolo and Canaletto, and the playwright Carlo Goldoni's new adaptations of *commedia dell'arte* broke exciting ground. If the city was a fading world power, it fast warmed to its new role as the playground of Europe, staging extravagant carnival balls and becoming notorious for gambling.

THE END OF THE REPUBLIC

Roughly 1,100 years on from its birth, the Venetian Republic came to end with the arrival of Napoleon in 1797. The last doge, Ludovico Manin, abdicated, the Great Council voted to dissolve itself, and the *Serenissima* was no more. After switching hands several times in the ensuing conflict, Venice became an Austrian possession after Waterloo, remaining so for over 50 years. Although the Austrians were despised by the Venetians, they did restore to the city most of the artistic booty taken by Napoleon. In 1846 they linked Venice to the mainland for the first time, erecting an unsightly railway bridge. In 1848, the Venetians rose up under revolutionary leader Daniele Manin and ousted the Austrian garrison; however, their provisional republic fell the following year. In 1866, after Austria's defeat by Prussia, the Venetians voted overwhelmingly to join the new Kingdom of Italy.

THE CITY TODAY

Venice remained largely unscathed by two world wars; more damaging was the pollution caused by an industrial port and oil refinery built at Porto Marghera in the 1920s. Equally serious was the severe flooding in November 1966, which led to the setting up of local and international organisations to restore Venetian artworks and palaces and to protect the city.

MOSE, Venice's controversial mobile flood barrier, is expected to be completed by the end of 2025, though it has already proven successful in protecting the city on numerous occurrences of *acqua alta* (high water). The Venice in Peril Fund (www.venicein-peril.org) supports the mobile barrier project, whilst admitting that it doesn't address the chronic issue of rising water levels, exacerbated by climate change. And as the need to deploy the barrier increases, so too does the risk of the lagoon's ecological degradation, cut off as it increasingly becomes from the natural flow of water.

NOTES

Until the late 17th century, the Palazzo Ducale was the only building in Venice that was allowed to be called a *palazzo*. Other splendid mansions were called simply Casa (house), shortened to Ca'. Many families did not bother to rename their houses *palazzi* once it was permitted, hence Ca' d'Oro, Ca' da Mosto and so on.

With or without MOSE, fears linger of Venice turning into the world's most famous fatality of climate change. Others, like writer Jonathan Keates, see chinks of hope: "Venice's very existence derives from a simple human yearning to make things happen against the odds."

CHRONOLOGY

6th century AD Refugees fleeing barbarians settle in the lagoon.

696 Election of Paoluccio Anafesto as the first doge.

829 The body of St Mark, stolen from Alexandria, is smuggled to Venice.

991–1008 Doge Pietro Orseolo II reigns. Commercial advantages are gained from Byzantium, and a sea battle is won against Dalmatia.

1104 The Arsenale is founded.

1202–4 Venice diverts the Fourth Crusade and sacks Constantinople.

1347–9 Nearly half the city's population wiped out by the Black Death.

1405 Venice takes Verona from Milan.

1423 Election of Doge Francesco Foscari begins Venetian expansion to Bergamo and Brescia and on to parts of Cremona.

1453 The Turks take Constantinople, heralding the expansion of the Ottoman Empire in Europe.

1571 Resounding victory against the Turks at Lepanto.

1797 Napoleonic troops enter Venice, and the Republic comes to an end.

1815 The Treaty of Vienna places the Veneto under Austrian control.

1848 Under Daniele Manin, Venice rebels against Austria.

1866 Venice becomes part of unified Italy.

1914–18 World War I. More than 600 bombs are dropped on Venice.

1966 Disastrous flooding leads to the launch of an international appeal.

1979 The Venice Carnival is revived and goes from strength to strength.

2008 The Calatrava Bridge is erected over the Grand Canal.

2009 The Punta della Dogana Contemporary Art Centre opens.

2013 The population of Venice falls to under 60,000.

2014 Venice's mayor Giorgio Orsoni and 35 others are put under arrest or investigation for allegedly siphoning off millions of euros from the MOSE flood barrier project.

MOSE flood barrier system

2018 Serious floods occur, with *acqua alta* (high water) of 156cm (5.1ft).

2021 Two years after a cruise ship crashes into a wharf, Venice instates a ban on large cruise ships (over 25,000 tonnes) sailing Venice's Giudecca Canal.

2022 The population of Venice falls to under 50,000 for the first time since the Middle Ages.

2025 MOSE, the system of 78 mobile dams, is due to be fully operational.

Gondola on a canal

Places

More like a stage set than a city, Venice has captivated visitors for centuries. *La Serenissima* dazzles and mesmerises, but also bewilders. Its singularity disorients the unprepared, but its uniqueness makes it a wonder of the world. Piazza San Marco is like a magnet, no matter your intention, you are inexorably drawn back, directed by the authoritative yellow *'per San Marco'* signs that mark the main thoroughfares. It is no hardship to return. The beautifully proportioned square that Napoleon termed 'the finest drawing room in Europe' is home to the great Basilica, the Doge's Palace and gracious cafés.

Venice is traditionally divided into six *sestieri* (districts). The obvious place to start is San Marco, with its famous church and piazza. To the east is Castello, home to several major churches and the Arsenale. South and west of San Marco, on the other side of the Grand Canal, is Dorsoduro with its art galleries, while inside the northern bend of the Grand Canal are San Polo and Santa Croce districts, centred on the Rialto. Finally, further north, with the train station and former Jewish Ghetto, is Cannaregio.

Stand on a little humpbacked bridge, far from the Grand Canal, and all you'll hear is the water lapping against the mossy walls, or the swish of a gondola that appears out of nowhere. Despite its watery character, most of the city is best explored on foot, with the occasional boat trip adding a new perspective or whisking you to the far corners of the lagoon.

SAN MARCO

HIGHLIGHTS

Basilica di San Marco

The magnet is always San Marco, home to several of the city's main landmarks. But do dip in and out of the square, as Venetians do, before exploring the rest of Venice. Despite its allure, this ceremonial district has little in common with the intimacy of other less well-known districts, let alone with the lagoon islands.

PIAZZA SAN MARCO

The main square in Venice, **Piazza San Marco ❶**, is a pulsating spot. The square was originally home to a monastic garden with a canal running through it, but since its transformation in the 12th and 13th centuries it has been the religious and political centre of the city. The Piazza has always pulled in the crowds – at the peak of the Republic's powers, some of the world's most spectacular processions, such as the one depicted in Gentile Bellini's celebrated painting at the Accademia (see page 58), were staged here. Victorious commanders returning home from the Genoese or Turkish wars were fêted in front of the Basilica with grand parades, while vendors on the square sold sweets and snacks, much as they do today. And under the arcades, Venetians and tourists have promenaded and been enchanted by elegant shops for centuries.

Yet despite all its pomp and circumstance and hustle and bustle, the Piazza remains a very civilised place. Dubbed by Napoleon the 'finest drawing room in Europe', it is elegantly proportioned, with colonnades on three sides, and fringed with exquisite monuments

THE LIONS OF VENICE

Pacific, playful or warlike, lions dominate paintings, sculptures, crests and illuminated manuscripts in Venice; they adorn buildings, bridges, balconies, archways and doorways, with the greatest concentration in the San Marco and Castello districts, closest to the centre of power. Whereas the seated lion represents the majesty of state, the walking lion symbolises Venetian sovereignty over its dominions. The Lion of St Mark bears a traditional greeting of peace and in times of war is depicted with a closed book, as in the arch over the Arsenale gateway. A few lions are shown clutching a drawn sword in one of their paws. The Napoleonic forces were well aware of the symbolism of lions and destroyed many prominent images; as a result, some, such as those on the Gothic gateway to the Palazzo Ducale, are replicas.

(most dating from the 16th and 17th centuries). Interestingly, the 'square' is actually a trapezoid, with uneven pavements sloping slightly downwards towards the Basilica. Its trachyte (volcanic rock) paving strips are more than 250 years old and lie over five or six earlier layers of tiles from the mid-13th century. Restoration works here in 2023 unearthed graves and traces of an early medieval church – possibly the original Church of San Geniniano, its final form razed in 1807 by Napoleon to make way for his **Ala Napoleonica**.

BASILICA DI SAN MARCO

Blending Eastern and Western elements, the **Basilica di San Marco** ❷ (St Mark's Basilica; www.basilicasanmarco.it; free; no large bags or backpacks allowed) is an exquisite, sumptuous shrine, encapsulating the old Republic's vision of itself as the successor to Constantinople. Despite the sloping irregular floors, an eclectic mix of styles both inside and out, the five low domes of totally unequal proportions and some 500 non-matching columns, San Marco still manages to convey a sense of grandeur as well as a jewel-like delicacy.

The church was originally built in AD 830 as a chapel for the doges and as a resting place for the remains of St Mark, which had just been stolen from Alexandria by two Venetian adventurers (see page 19). According to legend, they hid the body in a consignment of salted pork; Muslim customs officials, forbidden by their religion from eating or coming in contact with pork, did not do a thorough search and let the relics slip through their fingers. Not only were the body and many of the adornments in the Basilica stolen from the East but most of the church's columns were also brought back as booty from forays into the Levant.

NOTES

To avoid the long queues for the Basilica di San Marco reserve in advance at www.st-marks-basilica.com. Take your reservation to the special entrance for those with bookings.

The Basilica became the Republic's shrine as well as the coronation place of its doges. However, the original, largely wooden church burned down in 976, and the Basilica we see today was constructed between 1063 and 1094; its exterior was then lavishly decorated with marble and ornamentation over the next three centuries.

The narthex

The small porch at the entrance to the cathedral (the narthex) gives visitors their first sight of the fabulous **mosaics** that are a predominant feature of the

The Cavalli di San Marco, stolen from Constantinople

church's interior. Described by the poet W.B. Yeats as 'God's holy fire', they are said to cover a total area of around 0.5 hectares (1 acre). The narthex mosaics date from the 13th century and are among the most spectacular in the whole Basilica; they depict such Old Testament events as the Creation and the story of Noah's ark. The mosaics are at their best from 11.30am–12.45pm daily when the cathedral is illuminated.

Museo Marciano

The staircase immediately to the right of the main entrance leads to a small museum, the **Museo Marciano** (charge), housing some of the San Marco's finest treasures. The star attraction is the world's only surviving ancient *quadriga* (four horses abreast), known as

NOTES

Visitors in short skirts or shorts will not be allowed entry to Venice's churches, especially the Basilica di San Marco. Shoulders and backs must also be covered.

the **Cavalli di San Marco** (The Horses of St Mark) and cast around AD 200, either in Rome or Greece. At one time, the horses were believed to have crowned Trajan's Arch in Rome, but they were later moved to the imperial hippodrome in Constantinople, where Doge Dandolo claimed them as spoils of war in 1204, bringing them back to Venice. After guarding the shipyard of the Venetian Arsenale for a while, the *quadriga* was moved to the front of the cathedral, becoming almost as symbolic of the city as St Mark's trademark lion.

In 1378 the rival republic of Genoa boasted that it would 'bridle those unbridled horses', but it never succeeded. Napoleon managed to corral them, however, taking them to Paris to stand on the Place du Carrousel adjacent to the Louvre for 13 years. When Venice fell under Austrian rule, the Austrians restored the horses to San Marco, where they remained until World War I, when the Italian government moved them to Rome. During World War II they were moved again, this time into the nearby countryside. After the war, they were returned to the Basilica, although the ones on display at the front of the cathedral are only replicas – the original *quadriga* was moved inside to protect it against corrosion from air pollution. The Venetians have vowed that the horses will never be allowed to leave their city again.

The galleries in which the museums are situated provide good views of the interior; while outside on the Loggia dei Cavalli you can look down on Piazza San Marco and the adjacent *piazzetta*.

The Treasury and High Altar

Located just off the baptistery on the Basilica's right-hand side is the **Tesoro** (Treasury; charge), where you can see further riches looted from Constantinople at the time of the Fourth Crusade (1204). Close by is the **Altare Maggiore** (High Altar), which bears a *ciborium* (canopy) mounted on four alabaster columns dating from the 7th or 8th century; sculpted scenes from the lives of Christ and the Virgin Mary adorn the altar. In the illuminated grating is a sarcophagus containing the relics of St Mark.

The Pala d'Oro

Behind the altar is one of Christendom's greatest treasures, the **Pala d'Oro** (charge) a gold, bejewelled altar screen featuring dozens of scenes from the Bible. Originally crafted in the 12th century, the screen was embellished and enlarged on the doges' orders until it reached its present stage in the mid-14th century. Its exquisitely

Detail of the Pala d'Oro

wrought golden frame holds the Venetian equivalent of the Crown Jewels: 1,300 pearls, 400 garnets, 300 sapphires, 300 emeralds, 90 amethysts, 75 balas rubies, 15 rubies, four topazes and two cameos.

The only drawback to the fabulous splendour of the Pala d'Oro is that it attracts hordes of sightseers. The best way to try and beat the crowds is to visit either early in the morning, before day-trippers and tour groups have arrived, or late in the afternoon, after they have left.

CAMPANILE DI SAN MARCO

For breathtaking views of Piazza San Marco and the city, ascend the **Campanile di San Marco** (St Mark's Bell Tower; www.basilicasanmarco.it; charge), at 100m (335ft) Venice's tallest building, which over the years has served as a lighthouse, gun turret and belfry.

The Campanile

Within less than a minute a lift takes you to the top, where the exotic domes of the Basilica, the splendid wedge-shaped tip of the Dorsoduro (marking the start of the Grand Canal), the island church of San Giorgio Maggiore and the terracotta-coloured tiles of the ancient city roofscape are spread beneath your feet. The scene looks much the same now as it did over 200 years ago when the German writer J.W. von Goethe came here for his first view of the sea. It may well even look the same as four centuries ago when, according to local lore,

The gate to the Campanile

Galileo brought the doge up here to show off his new telescope. Intriguingly, not a single canal can be seen from the Campanile.

However, this most potent symbol of the city is not the original tower, which collapsed into the Piazza on 14 July 1902. Fortunately, the old building creaked and groaned so much in advance that everyone knew what was coming – numerous bell towers in Venice have fallen down over the centuries, so the locals were used to it and knew to keep their distance; the eventual collapse caused no injury. Contrary to the 'evidence' supplied on cleverly faked postcards on sale throughout the city, the moment was not caught on film.

The city council quickly decided to rebuild the bell tower 'as it was, where it was', and precisely 1,000 years after the erection of the original Campanile, on 25 April 1912 a new, lighter version was inaugurated. However, like many, this one is already starting to lean

---

WHERE TO SHOOT THE BEST PICTURES

Few cities see as many shutters click and, understandably, few locals as weary of tourists with cameras, obstructing bridges and narrow alleys. Photograph with respect, keeping elbows in check and ever mindful of the people around you.

Piazza San Marco offers plenty to photograph, whether focussed on the famous square's symmetry, crowds, towers or the storied basilica's bedazzled facade.

Ascend the **Campanile di San Marco** for one of Venice's best aerial views: San Marco's domes, the vast piazza and clear shots across the canal to San Giorgio Maggiore and the Basilica Santa Maria della Salute.

The view of the **Bridge of Sighs** (from the Riva's Ponte della Paglia|) and the **Rialto Bridge** (shot from the gondola docks on either side) are high among **Serenissima's** most cliched shots and for good reason. To avoid (contributing to) the crowds, shoot at dawn or dusk when the day-trippers have left.

Another breathtaking (if familiar) view to capture is from the **Accademia Bridge** – preferably in the early morning, when La Salute and the curve of the Grand Canal pop dramatically against the sunrise.

For Venice's celebrated gondoliers, it's hard to beat the vistas from the **Riva** just south of the Doge's Palace, crammed with mooring posts and framing San Giorgio Maggiore in the distant background.

PIAZZETTA DEI LEONCINI

The small square situated to the left as you face the Basilica is known as the **Piazzetta dei Leoncini**, after the two marble lions that have been here since 1722. On the side of the Basilica facing the Piazzetta is the tomb of Daniele Manin, the leader of Venice's revolt against Austria and the subsequent, short-lived Venetian Republic of 1848–9. A descendent of a family from the Venetian Ghetto, the heroic Manin was reinterred in this site of unequalled honour after the end of the Austrian Occupation in 1866, along with his wife and children – none of the doges were granted such a splendid resting place.

TORRE DELL'OROLOGIO

The Campanile is not the Piazza's only notable bell tower – the graceful **Torre dell'Orologio** (Clock Tower; www.visitmuve.it; tours by appointment only, 1–3 daily time slots between 11am and 4pm for English tours), features a splendid **zodiacal clock** that shows the time in both Arabic and Roman numerals and has been ticking for over 500 years. On Epiphany in January and through Ascension week in May three bright-eyed Magi and a trumpeting angel swing out from the face of the clock tower on the stroke of every hour and, stiffly bowing, ceremoniously rotate around a gilded Madonna.

Red marble lion in the Piazzetta dei Leoncini

St Mark's clock tower (Torre dell'Orologio)

At the top of the tower, two scantily clad North African bronze figures use hammers to strike a bell. According to Venetian legend, stroking the figures' exposed nether regions confers sexual potency for a year. Venetians also claim that a workman was knocked off the top of the tower in the 19th century by one of the hammers – perhaps a kind of revenge for the impertinence that the statues have to endure.

PROCURATIE VECCHIE AND NUOVE

Adjacent to the Torre dell'Orologio is the colonnaded **Procuratie Vecchie**, built in the 16th century as a home for the Procurators of San Marco (state officers charged with the administration of the *sestieri*, or Venetian districts). Below it is one of Venice's two most famous cafés, the Caffè Quadri (www.alajmo.it), favoured haunt of the Austrians during their occupation of the city in the 19th century.

The church of San Geminiano once stood at the far end of the Piazza opposite the Basilica, but in 1807 Napoleon ordered it to be demolished in order to make way for a wing joining the two sides of the square. On the facade of this wing, known as the **Ala Napoleonica** (Napoleon's Wing), there are several statues of Roman emperors and a central niche originally intended for a statue of Napoleon himself but pointedly left empty.

Opposite the Procuratie Vecchie is the **Procuratie Nuove**, built between 1582 and 1640 as a new home for the Procurators, and later occupied by Napoleon as a royal palace. The Museo Correr (see page 47) now occupies most of the upper floors of this building and the adjacent Ala Napoleonica. Below the Procuratie Nuove, on the side of the square facing Caffè Quadri, is the Piazza's other famous café, Florian (www.caffeflorian.com). Founded in 1720, but with a mid-19th-century interior, it may be the oldest continuously operating café in the world.

PALAZZO DUCALE

For nine centuries the magnificent **Palazzo Ducale ❸** (Doge's Palace; www.visitmuve.it; last entrance half an hour before closing

Palace facade

time; charge) was the seat of the Republic, serving as a council chamber, law court and prison, as well as the residence of most of Venice's doges. The Palazzo was first built in fortress-like Byzantine style in the 9th century and partially replaced 500 years later by a Gothic structure. The architects of this massive structure, with peach-and-white patterning in its brick facade, achieved an incredible delicacy by balancing the bulk of the building above two floors of Gothic arcades. The ravages inflicted by three devastating fires have necessitated some extensive reconstruction work over the centuries.

The palace's 15th-century ceremonial entrance, the **Porta della Carta** (Paper Gate), is a masterpiece of late Gothic stonework. Its name may derive from the fact that the doge's decrees were affixed here, or from the professional scribes who set up nearby. On the left, note the four curious figures of the Tetrarchs (also known as the 'Four Moors'), variously said to represent the Roman emperor Diocletian and associates, or four Saracen robbers who tried to loot the Basilica's *Treasury* through the wall behind them.

Visits start at the Porta del Frumento on the lagoon side of the palace. The **Museo dell' Opera** by the entrance houses some of the original carved capitals from the palazzo's loggias. Inside the courtyard is the impressive ceremonial stairway, the **Scala dei Giganti**, named after Sansovino's colossal statues of Neptune and Mars (symbolising, respectively, Venetian sea and land powers). Visitors use the only slightly less grandiose **Scala d'Oro** (Golden Staircase), which was built during the 16th century to designs by Jacopo Sansovino.

The interior

The main tour of the palace begins in the state rooms, in which the business of the Republic was once conducted. This part of the complex is home to some of the finest paintings in the ducal collection. On the walls in front of and behind you as you enter the **Anticollegio** are four allegories by Tintoretto, combining images of pagan gods and the four seasons to suggest that Venice is

The impressive Sala del Maggior Consiglio

favoured at all times. Jacob Bassano's *Jacob Returning to Canaan* is on the wall opposite the windows, on your right. To the left of it is Veronese's masterpiece, *The Rape of Europa*.

Proceed on to the **Sala del Collegio**, where the doges received ambassadors. Next is the **Sala del Senato** where the Venetian ruling council (made up of the doge, his advisors, members of the judiciary and senators) formulated policy.

The next room is the **Sala del Consiglio dei Dieci**, the meeting room of the Council of Ten. The Ten (who actually numbered up to 17) were a high-ranking group that met on matters of state security and acquired a reputation similar to that of the secret police. A letter box in the form of a lion's mouth, for the use of citizens who wished to inform the Ten of anything untoward, can be seen in the next room.

The Bridge of Sighs

On the public route, the palace's somewhat menacing aura is confirmed by a splendid private armoury, in which some extremely gruesome weapons are displayed.

The route then leads down to the first-floor state rooms. The most resplendent of all, is the **Sala del Maggior Consiglio** (Great Council Chamber), a vast hall where Venetian citizens assembled to elect doges and debate state policies in the early days of the Republic. Later, only the nobles convened here. The hall was built to hold an assembly of up to 1,700, but by the mid-16th century this figure had increased to around 2,500. Covering the whole of one end wall is Tintoretto's *Paradiso*, based on Dante's masterpiece, and undertaken by the artist (with the assistance of his son) while he was in his seventies. At 7m by 22m (23ft by 72ft), it is the largest old master oil painting in the world, containing some 350 human figures. Adorning the ceiling is Veronese's *Apotheosis of Venice*, which captures the ideal civic conception of Venice as serene, prosperous, elegant and self-assured. Portraits of 76 doges (several of which are little more than artistic guesswork) line the cornice beneath the ceiling. Conspicuously absent is the 14th-century doge, Marin Falier – a black veil marks his intended place of honour, and a notice tells us that he was beheaded for treason in 1355.

From here the tour takes you to the criminal courts and the Prigioni Nuove (New Prisons), which are reached by the legendary **Bridge of Sighs** (Ponte dei Sospiri). Teasingly, it was once dubbed 'bridge of signs' as it was shrouded in billboards for so long. Now restored, the baroque stone bridge, built in 1614, was given its more evocative name by Lord Byron who wrote: 'I stood in Venice on the Bridge of Sighs, a palace and a prison on each hand'. The idea that condemned prisoners sighed at their last glance of Venice when crossing the bridge derives more from romantic fiction than hard fact, as it was petty criminals who would have made the journey at that time. The bridge has two parallel passageways, each leading to different court and interrogation rooms, with small, dark cells on the other side, which are relatively civilised by medieval standards.

PIAZZETTA SAN MARCO

If Piazza San Marco is the drawing room of Venice, the smaller **Piazzetta San Marco** is its vestibule. The two soaring granite columns dominating the piazzetta were stolen from the East and hoisted upright here in 1172. They haven't moved since, although a third column apparently fell into the sea.

SECRET TOURS OF THE PALACE

The Itinerari Segreti is a fascinating guided tour (minimum two people; in English daily), which gives access to secret parts of the Doge's Palace that are normally off limits to visitors. The tour takes around 1 hour 15 minutes and includes the torture chamber and the cell from which Casanova, one of Venice's most notorious citizens, escaped in 1775. The tour ticket also gives access to the rest of the palace. Advance bookings can be made until two days before the visit (www.visitmuve.it) or, if still available, on the day by asking at the information desk.

On top of one of the columns is Venice's original patron saint, St Theodore; on the other stands what must be the strangest looking of the city's many stone lions – not really a lion at all but a *chimera*, a mythical hybrid beast (you can see it most clearly from the balcony of the Palazzo Ducale). Even though its exact origin is unknown, it is thought to be of Eastern provenance and may be up to 2,200 years old.

Nowadays the area is a lively hub bustling with tourists but stepping back in time between the 15th and mid-18th centuries, it was a place of execution. One of the more creative punishments involved torturing the prisoner, burning them on a raft, dragging them through the streets and finally putting them to death between the columns.

Café Florian, Piazza di San Marco

MUSEO CORRER AND MUSEO ARCHEOLOGICO

There are two museums on Piazza San Marco, both of which are usually not too crowded. The **Museo Correr** ❹ (www.visitmuve. it; last entrance half an hour before closing time; charge) occupies some 70 rooms of the Ala Napoleonica and Procuratie Nuove. It is home to the city museum and contains artefacts from virtually every aspect of Venice's history. It houses a fine collection of 14th- to 16th-century Venetian paintings, including a room of works by Jacopo Bellini and his sons, Giovanni and Gentile. Vittorie Carpaccio's *Two Venetian Noblewomen*, traditionally and erroneously known as *The Courtesans*, is also displayed here. Other highlights include sculpture by Canova, wonderful old globes and incredible stilt-like platform shoes worn by 15th-century Venetian courtesans.

The **Museo Archeologico** (Archaeological Museum; https://archeologicovenezia.cultura.gov.it; charge), is accessed through Museo Correr. It occupies part of the lavish 16th-century building opposite the Palazzo Ducale on Piazzetta San Marco. The core collection here consists of Greek and Roman sculpture bequeathed by Cardinal Grimani in 1523, a gift that influenced generations of Venetian artists who came to study here. Among the Roman busts, medals, coins, cameos and portraits are Greek originals and Roman copies, including a 5th-century Hellenistic *Persephone*.

NOTES

Keen sightseers can cut costs by purchasing a San Marco Square Museum Ticket at www.visitmuve.it. This covers the Doge's Palace, Museo Correr, Museo Archeologico and Biblioteca Marciana. Alternatively, for a slightly higher price, you could opt for the Musei Civici's cumulative Museum Pass (same website), covering the museums on San Marco Square plus a dozen others across Venice.

BIBLIOTECA MARCIANA

In the other part of the building opposite the Palazzo Ducale, and likewise accessed through Museo Correr, is the **Biblioteca Nazionale Marciana** (National Library of St Mark; https://bibliotecanazionalemarciana.cultura.gov.it; closed Sun), also known as the Libreria Sansoviniana after its architect Jacopo Sansovino. Palladio described it as 'the richest building since antiquity'. The magnificent main hall of the original library is decorated with paintings by Veronese, Tintoretto and other leading artists of the time.

Just a few yards behind the library are the **Giardinetti Reali** (Royal Gardens). The best tourist information office (see page 137) is in the neighbouring Venice Pavilion, with another at the southwest exit of Piazza San Marco.

The perfectly proportioned Scala del Bovolo

ALSO IN SAN MARCO

If you have more time to explore San Marco *sestiere*, there is an intriguing tower, an opera house and a Gothic church within a few minutes' walk of Piazza San Marco.

Hidden in a maze of alleys between Calle Vida and Calle Contarini, close to Campo Manin, is **Palazzo Contarini del Bovolo** (www.gioiellinascostidivenezia.it; charge), a late-Gothic palace renowned for its romantic arcaded staircase, the **Scala del Bovolo** ❺.

A gondola gliding through the Venetian canals

Bovolo means 'snail-shell' in Venetian dialect and fittingly describes this graceful external spiral staircase, which is linked to loggias of brick and smooth white stone.

La Fenice (www.teatrolafenice.it; charge), the city's main opera house, is located on Campo San Fantin, west of Piazza San Marco. One of the world's loveliest opera auditoria, it was almost completely destroyed by fire in 1838, but rose again 'like a phoenix' *(fenice)*, rebuilt almost exactly. After fire struck again in 1996, the theatre has once again been restored to its former glory and the latest fire precautions installed.

The Gothic **Santo Stefano** church (www.chorusvenezia.org; charge), located on Campo Santo Stefano, west of the opera house, is a large, airy structure decorated with rich ornamentation and works by Tintoretto.

CASTELLO

HIGHLIGHTS

The eastern region of Venice, Castello is the largest of the city's *sestieri*. The name derives from a former 8th century castle built on the island of San Pietro in the east. Castello is home to the Arsenale, where the great Venetian galleys were built, the fine Gothic church of Santi Giovanni e Paolo and the Scuola di San Giorgio degli Schiavoni with its exquisite frieze of paintings by Carpaccio.

ALONG THE WATERFRONT

There are few more stately waterfronts in the world than that of Venice's splendid *riva* (quay), which curves gently away from San Marco towards the *sestiere* of Castello. The first section, the **Riva degli Schiavoni** (Quay of the Slavs), begins in front of the Palazzo Ducale. The bustling quay takes its name from the Dalmatian merchants who used to tie up their boats here – vessels laden with wares from the East. This is still a cosmopolitan spot, though less exotic than in its heyday. Boats still moor here, too: *vaporetti* (waterbuses or ferries) at the busy landing stage of San Zaccaria and fleets of gondolas waiting to tempt tourists.

East of the Palazzo Ducale, the next sight you'll see (with your back to the waterfront) is the Bridge of Sighs. A little further on is the red **Palazzo Dandolo**, now the legendary **Hotel Danieli** (www.hoteldanieli.com), with a lavish neo-Gothic lobby. When Proust stayed here, he declared, 'When I went to Venice, I found that my dream had become – incredibly but quite simply – my address'. The Danieli was also the scene of an unhappy love affair between the writers George Sand and Alfred de Musset in 1883.

A little further on, after the colonnaded Ponte del Vin, the second turning to the left leads away from the waterfront to a quiet *campo* overlooked by the splendid 16th-century church of **San Zaccaria ❻** (free; crypt: charge). Supposedly the last resting place of Zaccharias (the father of John the Baptist), whose body lies in the right aisle, this Gothic-Renaissance masterpiece features Giovanni Bellini's celebrated *Madonna and Child*. The side chapels have splendid glowing altarpieces, and the eerie, permanently

The view around Arsenale

Lion guarding the Arsenale

flooded 9th-century crypt, where several early doges rest in watery graves, is one of the most atmospheric spots in the city.

Back on the waterfront, continue eastwards for the church of **La Pietà** (www.pietavenezia.org; charge), a handsome building with a fine ceiling painting by Giambattista Tiepolo. It is known as 'Vivaldi's church', after Antonio Vivaldi who was concertmaster here from 1705 to 1740.

Carry on past the statue of King Vittorio Emanuele II and you'll notice the crowds starting to thin out. By the time you reach the Arsenale *vaporetto* stop, just a short distance from the Palazzo Ducale, the crowds will probably have dispersed completely, even in high season.

THE ARSENALE

For 700 years, before Napoleon's invasion in the late 18th century, the Republic's galleys and galleons were built at the **Arsenale ❼** (guided tours by appointment only during La Biennale; tel: 041-521 8828), once the greatest shipyard in the world. Dante visited it, and used the images of its workers toiling amid cauldrons of boiling pitch as the inspiration for his *Inferno*. *Arsenale*, originally from the Arabic for 'house of industry', is one of those Venetian coinages that have passed into universal usage. The yard also originated the concept of the assembly line. Output was prodigious.

One of the yard's proudest achievements came in 1574, while Henri III of France was visiting Venice. In the time it took for the French king to get through his state banquet at the Palazzo Ducale, the workers at the Arsenale had constructed a fully equipped galley from scratch, ready for the king's inspection.

Today, there's little to remind visitors of those heady days. Napoleon destroyed the Arsenale in 1797, and although it was rebuilt by the Austrians, operations here ceased in 1917. The shipyard is now mainly used by the navy, and as the nerve centre for the building of MOSE, the mobile barrier. Some sections serve as art exhibition spaces during La Biennale (see box) and as venues for concerts. At the entrance visitors can only admire the impressive 15th-century gateway, guarded by a motley collection of white stone lions, all stolen from ancient Greek sites. The two on the river side are believed to date back to the 6th century BC.

MUSEO STORICO NAVALE

The nearest you will get to the spirit of the age is in the **Museo Storico Navale** (Naval History Museum; www.munav.it; charge). For

---

LA BIENNALE

Established in 1895, Venice's Biennale (www.labiennale.org) is one of the oldest, most important contemporary art jamborees in the world. Nowadays (since a COVID-19 postponement), it takes place in even numbered years, (the architectural Biennale is held on odd years) from late spring or early summer until November. It is held in several main locations – in the Arsenale, where the restored Corderie (rope factory) is the main venue, and in the Giardini Pubblici, where there are around 40 pavilions. Each pavilion is sponsored by a different country, offering a chance for avant-garde art, often with wry political comment. Elsewhere, on the Zattere waterfront behind La Salute, the former salt warehouses have become another showcase for contemporary art.

many visitors the star attraction is the model of the last *Bucintoro*, the gilded barge that was used by the doge on state occasions, although entire sections of other state barges and warships are also on show.

Whether heading for the Biennale exhibition or just wandering, it's worth coming this far simply for the splendid views back towards the Palazzo Ducale. Sightseeing as such is subservient to waterfront charm in the untouristy neighbourhood of Eastern Castello.

SCUOLA DI SAN GIORGIO DEGLI SCHIAVONI

Returning to La Pietà, take the alley beside the church, turn right at Salizzada dei Greci and left after the canal for the **Scuola di San Giorgio degli Schiavoni** (www.scuoladalmatavenezia.com; closed Tues; charge). The five Venetian *scuole* were craft guilds of laymen under the banner of a particular saint, and this one was founded in 1451 as the guildhall of the city's Dalmatian merchants. In the early 16th century these Slavs *(Schiavoni)*, prospering from trade with the East, commissioned Vittorio Carpaccio to decorate their hall. His nine richly detailed panels, completed between 1502 and 1508, decorate the lower floor and depict the lives of the three Dalmatian patron saints: Jerome, Tryphone and George. Note Carpaccio's gory *St George and the Dragon*.

SANTA MARIA FORMOSA

Return to Salizzada dei Greci and follow the flow west across the Rio dei Greci for the Fondamenta dell'Osmarin. A right turn at the Ponte dei Carmini and along Calle Rota will take you up to the lively **Campo Santa Maria Formosa** where the 15th-century church of the same name (https://santamariaformosa.it), is noted for its altarpiece by Palma il Vecchio.

SANTI GIOVANNI E PAOLO (SAN ZANIPOLO)

Commonly known as **San Zanipolo ❽** (names are often slurred together in the Venetian dialect), this church (www.

santigiovanniepaolo.it; charge) is one of the largest in Venice after San Marco, disputing second place with its great Gothic sister, the Frari (see page 73). The church is located on Campo Santi Giovanni e Paolo, north of Campo Santa Maria Formosa, reached via the café-lined Calle Lunga Santa Maria Formosa. The huge brick church was completed in 1430 for the Dominican Order and is known nowadays as Venice's Pantheon, as such a large number of doges (25 in all) and dignitaries of the Republic lie within. Like the Frari, the church is cavernous, with graphic sculptures adorning its tombs. The church's treasures include an early polyptych by Giovanni Bellini in the right-hand nave.

San Zanipolo shares the *campo* with the striking, marble facade of the late 15th-century **Scuola Grande di San Marco** (a civic

Stalls in Campo Santa Maria Formosa

hospital housing a small medical museum; www.scuolagrande-sanmarco.it; closed Sun, Mon; charge). Straight ahead is the magnificent, 15th-century equestrian **statue of Bartolomeo Colleoni** by Andrea Verrochio and Alessandro Leopardi. The subject is the mercenary military leader who worked in the service of Venice for many years and left a large legacy to the city on condition that his statue would be raised 'on the Square of San Marco'. The leaders of the Republic, who had never erected statues to any of their leaders or permitted cults of personality, wanted the legacy but could not conceive of erecting a statue to a mercenary soldier in Piazza San Marco. As a compromise, Colleoni's statue was placed in the square of the Scuola Grande di San Marco – the rather tenuous San Marco association presumably saved the municipal conscience.

Santa Maria dei Miracoli

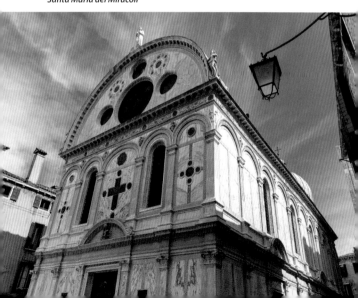

SANTA MARIA DEI MIRACOLI

West of Santi Giovanni e Paolo, hidden amid a warren of canals and houses, lies the beautifully restored church of **Santa Maria dei Miracoli** (www.chorusvenezia.org; charge) a popular choice for Venetian weddings. Built from 1481 to 1489 by the Lombardo family of inventive stonemasons who also created the trompe-l'œil facade of the Scuola Grande di San Marco, the church has exquisite marble veneers on its inner and outer walls and an arched ceiling decorated with 50 portraits of prophets and saints.

DORSODURO

HIGHLIGHTS

Dorsoduro encompasses the section of Venice that lies just across the Grand Canal from San Marco. Although the name 'Dorsoduro' might not be instantly recognisable to many first-time visitors, most will fall for this picturesque *sestiere*. It is home to Venice's finest art gallery, the Accademia, and to the iconic Santa Maria della Salute Basilica.

Chic Dorsoduro is the artiest *sestiere*, with beguiling walks along the Zattere quayside, and bohemian backwaters with a gondola boatyard and earthy Giudecca counterpointed by the grandstanding art and architecture of La Salute, the Accademia and the Guggenheim collection.

Scuola Grande di San Rocco

THE ACCADEMIA

The **Gallerie dell'Accademia** ❾ (www.gallerieaccademia. it/en; charge) is home to the greatest collection of Venetian art and is the most-visited spot in the city after Piazza San Marco and the Palazzo Ducale. A maximum of 180 visitors are allowed in at any one time, so arrive early to avoid the queues or make a reservation.

The collection spans paintings from the 14th to the 18th centuries, arranged roughly chronologically beginning with the first floor and continuing to the ground floor. But be selective and focus on the museum's highlights at least.

At the time of writing, some of the final rooms of the Accademia's first floor remained closed for renovations, among them Room XX. Traditionally, this room has housed Venetian treasures such as Bellini's celebrated *Procession around the Piazza Bearing the Cross* and Carpaccio's epic *Miracle of the Holy Cross at the Rialto Bridge* which are currently being restored. Occupying a spacious loft atop a church contained within the gallery structure, Room XXIII also remains closed. Please note that due to the frequent rearrangement of artwork, the location of paintings may also be subject to change - check the Accademia website beforehand.

A visit begins up the grand double staircase from the entrance in the wonderfully restored Sala del Capitolo, the confraternity hall, overlooked by hundreds of winged angels adorning the ceiling and filled with 15th-century devotional pieces.

Breaking into the 16th century, **Hall III** contains a fine series by Jacopo Bellini and his sons Giovanni and Gentile, continuing over several rooms and including Gentile's faded but powerful *Blessed Lorenzo Giustinian* (usually displayed in Room XXIII). Among others of the artist's works, Carpaccio's striking *Crucifixion of the Ten*

VENETIAN ARTISTS

Jacopo Bellini (1400–70) and his sons **Giovanni** (1430–1516) and **Gentile** (1429–1507) inaugurated the *Serenissima's* glorious era of art in the 15th century.

The Venetian High Renaissance began with **Giorgione** (*c.*1477–1510), whose great promise can be seen in *Tempest*, at the Accademia.

Vittore Carpaccio (1445–1526) painted detailed scenes of city life as well as the splendid series on the life of St Ursula at the Accademia.

Titian (1490–1576) was widely hailed as the finest painter of his era. Only a few of his works can be seen in Venice; these include the *Assumption of the Virgin*, above the altar of the Frari church.

Jacopo Tintoretto (1518–94) was a quiet, religious man who left Venice only once. Most of his work remains in the city. See his genius in the Scuola di San Rocco and his parish church of Madonna dell'Orto.

Paolo Veronese (1528–88) is inextricably linked with the church of San Sebastiano, which is resplendent with his paintings. Many of his works are in the Accademia.

Antonio Canaletto (1697–1768) is famed for his detailed paintings of Venice but only a handful are on show in the city – most were sold abroad by his English patron, Josef Smith.

Perhaps the greatest Venetian decorative painter was **Giovanni Battista Tiepolo** (1696–1770), who covered the ceiling of the upper hall in the Scuola Grande dei Carmini with nine masterly paintings.

Thousand Martyrs is displayed in **Hall II**. **Hall XXI** typically houses the latter's lyrical, poetically narrative *St Ursula* cycle, which depicts the tragic life of this Breton heroine. It spans her acceptance of the hand of the British prince, Hereus, on condition of his conversion to Christianity, to their subsequent pilgrimage to Rome and eventual martyrdom at the hands of Attila the Hun. At the time of writing, restorations to Hall XXI were ongoing and most works by Vittore Carpaccio were not on display. However, you should check the official Accademia website for the latest information.

Highlights of **Halls IV** and **VI b** include Mantegna's *St George* and Giovanni Bellini's *Martyrdom of St Mark*, completed with the help of Vittore Belliniano and straddling the doorway between the two rooms. **Hall VII** is graced by works of the great Flemish artist Hieronymus Bosch, among them his poignantly brooding panels, *The Visions of the Hereafter*.

'The Feast in the House of Levi' at the Gallerie dell'Accademia

Hall VIII holds the most famous work of art in the gallery, Giorgione's moody and enigmatic *Tempest*; it also houses *The Old Woman*, by the same artist.

In **Hall X** look out for Veronese's *Feast at the House of Levi*, a painting of a raucous Renaissance banquet originally entitled (and meant to depict) *The Last Supper*. When church officials condemned the work as sacrilegious and ordered Veronese to change it, he blithely did nothing but change its name.

Hall XI features Jacopo Tintoretto's dazzling St Mark paintings, notably the haunting *Removal of the Body of St Mark*. Here you'll also find Titian's dark *Pietà*, the artist's last work, intended for his tomb.

The ground floor rooms feature many fine works by Tiepolo, among them his *Rape of Europa (Hall VI)* along with several prized *capricci* by Canaletto (Hall VIII).

Alexander Calder sculpture 'The Cow' at the Peggy Guggenheim Collection

COLLEZIONE PEGGY GUGGENHEIM

Just to the east of the Accademia along the Grand Canal, in the Palazzo Venier dei Leoni, is another exceptional museum, the **Collezione Peggy Guggenheim** ❿ (www.guggenheim-venice.it; closed Tues; charge), which is generally regarded as one of the best modern art collections in Europe. The bequest of American expatriate and heiress Peggy Guggenheim, who died in 1979, is displayed in the building she made her home: an eccentrically designed, one-storey 18th-century palace (still unfinished), with its gardens and terrace overlooking the Grand Canal. Guggenheim was renowned for her hospitality, and the museum stages regular events, from late openings to concerts and drinks parties. The welcoming museum café, with a menu designed by the owner of Ai Gondolieri, is also

one of the better restaurants in Venice.

Among the outstanding exhibits are early Picassos and Chagalls and Brancusi's bronze sculpture *Maiastra*. Other highlights include works by Max Ernst (whom Guggenheim married), Dalí, Miró, Piet Mondrian and Jackson Pollock, as well as a sculpture by Calder that Guggenheim used in lieu of a headboard for her bed. Sculptures by Giacometti dot the garden. Don't miss Marino Marini's *Angel of the City*, a bronze equestrian statue in the garden facing the Grand Canal.

A beautiful view of Canal Grande and Basilica di Santa Maria della Salute

LA SALUTE

Having presided over the entrance to the Grand Canal for over 300 years, the magnificent baroque church of **Santa Maria della Salute** ⑪ (https://basilicasalutevenezia.it; free) is almost as famil-iar a Venetian landmark as the Basilica di San Marco. The church, popularly known among the Venetians as 'La Salute', was built as an offering of thanks to the Virgin Mary for the end of a catastrophic plague in 1630 – the plague wiped out over a third of the lagoon's inhabitants. Under the direction of the young architect, Baldassare Longhena, construction began in 1631 and more than one million oak pilings were sunk into the swampy earth to support the mas-sive structure. Longhena lived to see the church, his life's work, completed in 1682. Each year, on 21 November, the church's feast day (Festa della Salute), engineers build a great pontoon of boats over the Grand Canal, and most of the city's population, resident and visiting, join a procession across the water and into the church. This is the only day that the church's main doors are opened.

While you're free to admire the major rotunda from inside, a ticket is required to glimpse the treasures of the **sacristy**, to the left of the high altar.

Among these are Tintoretto's magnificent painting of the *Marriage at Cana* and three Titians (*Cain and Abel, Abraham Sacrificing Isaac* and *David and Goliath*). A separate ticket will grant you roof access where you can admire panoramic views from atop the church's dome.

The Punta della Dogana Contemporary Art Centre

DOGANA

Continue east from the Salute towards the tip of Dorsoduro. At this point you'll find the 17th-century **Dogana da Mar** (Customs House), where the cargoes from all incoming ships were inspected in former days. The long-abandoned building has been converted by Japanese architect, Tadao Ando, into the **Punta della Dogana Contemporary Art Centre** (www.pinaultcollection.com; closed Tues; charge with combined ticket) with rotating displays of art-works from the world-class collection of François Pinault, owner of the Palazzo Grassi (see page 85). Designed like a ship's prow, this 17th-century Customs House is crowned by two bronze Atlas figures bearing a golden globe, with the weathervane figure of Fortuna on top. Striking contemporary sculptures also adorn the quaysides, notably the *Boy with Frog* who is perched on the point, and a bold

GONDOLAS AND GONDOLIERS

Nothing is more quintessentially Venetian than the gondola, although nowadays they are more a tourist attraction than a means of transportation. Gondolas have existed since the 11th century, and in the 18th century around 14,000 plied Venice's canals; today, the number has fallen to 400.

All gondolas are made to the same specifications, built by hand from around 280 separate pieces of wood. Curiously, they are asymmetrical (the left side is wider than the right) in order to accommodate the gondolier as he rows and steers. Gondolas are painted black in deference to the sumptuary laws of 1562 that attempted to curb the extravagances of Venetian society. They also retain a rather curious metallic pronged prow (or *ferro*). Several explanations have been offered for the symbolism and shape of the *ferro*: some think that the blades represent the six districts of Venice; others maintain that the shape suggests the Grand Canal or even the doge's cap.

Many gondoliers still wear the traditional outfit of straw boater, striped T-shirt and white sailor's top.

talking point on the Zattere side, part installation, part hoist.

Lap up the views from here, looking straight into the Bacino di San Marco (St Mark's Basin) in one direction and across the **Canale della Giudecca** (Giudecca Canal) in the other. The vista takes in the islands of Giudecca and San Giorgio Maggiore, including three churches designed by Andrea Palladio: the imposing **San Giorgio Maggiore** (see page 86); **Le Zitelle** (the Church of the Spinsters); and the landmark **Redentore** (Redeemer). The

Classic gondolier garb

last was built, like the Salute after it, as an act of thanksgiving at the end of the devastating plague of 1575–6. As at the Salute, there is an annual celebration at the Redentore each third Sunday of July; the festivities end with a flotilla of small boats and a firework display over the water.

ZATTERE

The **Fondamente delle Zattere** (Quay of the Rafts), runs all the way along the southern waterfront from the Dogana to the Rio di San Sebastiano. The floating rafts that gave the Zattere its name were once major unloading points for cargoes of salt. The huge salt warehouse, once capable of storing over 40,000 tons of the mineral, now doubles as an exhibition centre and as a boathouse for a local rowing club.

Continue along the Zattere past the churches of Spirito Santo and the Gesuati (Santa Maria del Rosario). Turn right on to the Fondamenta Nani and you'll see the rustic **Squero di San Trovaso** on the other side (*squero* means boatyard). In the 16th century, when thousands of gondolas plied the waters, there were many *squeri*; nowadays, San Trovaso is the only one where you can see gondolas repaired. The church of **San Trovaso** (chorusvenezia.org; charge) is worth investigating for two of Tintoretto's last works, both completed by his son.

Head back to the Zattere, which, with its cafés and restaurants, is a good place to take a break. The huge red-brick landmark that you can see across the water right at the western end of Giudecca is the **Molino Stucky**, a flour mill that was part of an attempt to bring modern industry to Venice in the 1890s. Now reborn as the Hilton Molino Stucky, the hotel has ravishing rooftop views, a swimming pool, and Skyline, an exciting rooftop cocktail bar.

GIUDECCA

When you have time, cross over to **Giudecca**, Venice's most diverse neighbourhood, where palatial hotels like the Hilton Molino Stucky are cheek by jowl with authentic inns, a boatyard and earthy working-class bars.

Giudecca feels like a thriving community, with arty incomers living beside gondola-makers, boat-repairers, sailors, celebrities and craftspeople. When monumental Venice palls, or the crowds feel overwhelming, just hop on a ferry to Giudecca for an unfussy lunch and views or for sunset wanderings and cocktails.

For now, turn right along the Zattere waterfront and, at the San Basilio landing stage, head inland, following the canal north. Cross the tiny bridge for the splendid 16th-century church of **San Sebastiano** (chorusvenezia.org; charge). It is a tribute to Veronese, who painted most of the opulent works decorating the walls, altar and ceiling from 1555 to 1565. The artist is also buried here.

Dining in Campo Santa Margherita Square

The next square west is Campo Angelo Raffaele, named after its 17th century church. The adjoining canal leads to the humble parish church of **San Nicolò dei Mendicoli** (free) – often overlooked, but its modest exterior belies its lavishly decorated interior. The church was founded in the 7th century, making it one of the oldest in the city, and remodelled between the 12th and 14th centuries; it was restored in 1977 by the Venice in Peril Fund (www.veniceinperil. org). The church's single nave is graced by Romanesque columns, Gothic capitals and beamed ceilings, and adorned by Renaissance panelling, gilded statuary and School of Veronese paintings.

THE UNIVERSITY QUARTER

The attractive area between the Accademia and Campo Santa Margherita is popular with students and younger visitors. In term time **Campo Santa Margherita** ⑫, home to bars, inns, bohemian shops and colourful market stalls, is the liveliest square in Venice outside Piazza San Marco. At one end of the square is the deconsecrated church of **Santa Margherita**, now a beautiful auditorium belonging to the university, while at the other end is the spacious and ornately decorated **Chiesa dei Carmini** (Church of the Carmelites; charge). For even more religious art, call in next door at **I Carmini** (www.scuolagrandecarmini.it; charge), the headquarters of the Scuola Grande dei Carmini and a showcase to Tiepolo, who covered the ceiling of the Upper Hall with nine paintings, the last one completed in 1744.

From Campo Santa Margherita the Rio Terrà street leads southeast towards **Campo San Barnaba** which sits on the other side of San Barnaba canal. Here you'll see an attractive fruit-and-vegetable barge moored along the quay, and the solemn, Neoclassical church of **San Barnaba** (www.leonardoavenezia.com; charge), which film buffs may recognise as the setting for major scenes in *Summertime* (1955) starring Katharine Hepburn, and *Indiana Jones and the Last Crusade* (1989) with Harrison Ford. Now a museum, the former church is crammed with various inventions of Leonardo da Vinci.

CA' REZZONICO

On the other side of the San Barnaba canal where it meets the Grand Canal is the glorious 17th-century **Ca' Rezzonico** ⑬ (www.visitmuve.it; closed Tues; charge), home to the **Museo del Settecento Veneziano** (Museum of 18th-Century Venice), another of Dorsoduro's major art collections. Here, however, the 17th-century palatial setting is just as important as the 18th-century exhibits it houses.

Stepping into the Ca' Rezzonico is a feast for the eyes. At the top of the vast entrance staircase is a ballroom, featuring two immense Murano-glass chandeliers as well as decorated ceilings and walls. In the adjacent room are intricately carved figures of chained slaves.

Ceilings by Tiepolo (father and son) are the main artistic interest until you reach the gallery on the second floor. Most visitors are drawn to the two Canaletto paintings of the Grand Canal – there are only a handful of paintings by him in the whole of Venice. You'll also find works by Pietro Longhi, who recorded the final, decadent century of the Venetian Republic. On the third and fourth floors of the museum, the Gallery Egidio Martini showcases an impressive collection of around 300 works, mainly by Venetian painters.

The Throne Room, Ca' Rezzonico

The views from the windows overlooking the Grand Canal are also to be savoured. Pen Browning, the son of poet Robert Browning, owned this palace in the late 19th century and his father died here in 1889.

SAN POLO AND SANTA CROCE

HIGHLIGHTS

The two adjoining *sestieri* of San Polo and Santa Croce are curved into the left bank of the Grand Canal. Together they are home to many important sights, including the artistic treasure houses of the church of the Frari and the Scuola Grande di San Rocco, as well as one of the city's most vibrant markets, on the Rialto.

THE RIALTO

Not only Venice's oldest district, the **Rialto** is also the area with the greatest concentration of Veneto-Byzantine palaces. From its earliest foundation, this was the powerhouse of the Republic, and a crossroads between the East and the West. On a practical level, it also acted as a busy commercial exchange and meeting place for merchants. As such, it is often described as 'Venice's kitchen, office

Ponte di Rialto

and back parlour'. During the peak of the Republic's influence it was one of the most important financial centres in Europe.

Ponte di Rialto

The **Ponte di Rialto** ⑭ (Rialto Bridge) divides the city into two, with the right bank, on the San Marco side, known as the *Rialto di quà* (this side), and the left bank known as the *Rialto di là* (that side). The bridge spans the Grand Canal with a strong, elegantly curved arch of marble, and is lined with shops selling silk ties, scarves, leather and jewellery. Henry James appreciated the 'small shops and booths that abound in Venetian character' but also felt 'the communication of insect life'.

The current bridge is merely the last in a line that began with simple pontoons and then progressed to a wooden structure, with a drawbridge section to allow the passage of tall ships. A new bridge was created in 1588–91 by Antonio da Ponte following the collapse of the previous one. Tradition has it that the greatest architects of the day, including Michelangelo and Palladio, competed for the commission, but da Ponte's design was chosen. The result is a light, floating structure with shops nestling in its solid, closed arches. From the bridge one can admire the majestic sweep of palaces and warehouses swinging away to La Volta del Canal, the great elbow-like bend in the Grand Canal.

The Rialto markets

The **Rialto markets** ⑮ make a refreshing change from the monumental Venice of San Marco. Ignore the tourist tat in favour of foodstuffs galore – and forays to traditional or contemporary *bacari* (Venetian wine and tapas bars). These serve anything from sushi to asparagus parcels or baby artichokes, salt cod or meatballs.

The **Erberia** is a fruit-and-vegetable market overlooking the Grand Canal. Casanova relished its 'innocent pleasure', but latter-day foodies find pleasure in the profusion of herbs, flowers, fruit, Veneto wines and vegetables.

The markets extend along the bank to the **Pescheria**, the fish market, set in an arcaded neo-Gothic hall by the quayside, a design inspired by Carpaccio's realistic paintings. Under the porticoes, fishermen display their catch on mountains of ice. The adjoining **Campo delle Beccarie**, once a public abattoir, now contains market overspill and lively foodie bars.

CAMPO SAN POLO

The biggest square in the city outside Piazza San Marco, **Campo San Polo** is notable for its church and for the mid-14th-century rose-coloured **Palazzo Soranzo**, situated just opposite. Casanova came to this palace in the 18th century as a young, hired violinist, living as the adopted son and heir to the family fortune with an

The Frari is Venice's largest Gothic church

entrée to Venetian society. From here, he went on to seduce and outrage Europe's 18th-century aristocracy.

Note the fine portal of the church of **San Polo** ⓰ (chorusven-ezia.org; charge), one of the few features that survives from the original 15th-century building. The interior, reached through a side door, features a brooding *Last Supper* by Tintoretto and Giandomenico Tiepolo's *Via Crucis (Stations of the Cross)* painted when he was only 20 years old. A campanile, dating from 1362, stands a short way from the church and is adorned with two of the Republic's less-appealing lions, one playing with a human head, the other with a serpent.

THE FRARI

Santa Maria Gloriosa dei Frari ⓱ (known simply as the Frari, a deformation of *frati*, meaning 'brothers'; www.basilicadeifrari.it; charge) is Venice's second church after San Marco and the resting place of the painter Titian. The brothers in question – members of the Franciscan order – were granted a piece of land in 1236, and the church, a huge lofty structure, was rebuilt between 1340 and 1469.

The church's greatest treasure is the soaring, mysterious *Assumption* (1518) hanging in the Gothic apse above the high altar. One of Titian's early masterpieces, this painting helped to establish his reputation. To the right is Donatello's much-admired wooden statue of *St John the Baptist*. Restored during the 19th century, it is the Florentine artist's sole remaining work in Venice. Tucked away in the sacristy on the right is the *Madonna and Saints* (1488), a trip-tych by Giovanni Bellini. Don't miss the beautiful marquetry and intricate carving on the choir stalls – this choir is one of the few in Venetian churches to stand in its original location.

The Frari is also notable for its huge monuments to Titian and to the 19th-century sculptor, Canova, on opposite sides of the great nave. Although Titian was buried here in 1576, the monument to him was not built until the mid-19th century. Canova's pyramidical cenotaph was erected in 1827, five years after his death. In 2022, exactly 200 years after his passing, the water-damaged structure was restored by the Venice in Peril Fund. While most of the beloved Neoclassicist's remains are interred in his hometown of Passagno, his heart rests here.

Several doges are entombed in the Frari, including two in the high altar. The church is also home to one of the city's most bombastic monuments, which is dedicated to Doge Giovanni Pesaro and situated next to Canova's mausoleum.

SCUOLA GRANDE DI SAN ROCCO

The nearby **Scuola Grande di San Rocco** ⑱ (www.scuolagrande-sanrocco.it; charge) stirs the emotions. John Ruskin, the foremost Venetian art historian of the 19th century and one of the city's most scrupulous observers, described San Rocco as having one of the three most precious picture collections in all of Italy. The novelist Henry James was also a devotee, although he found the Scuola Grande a little too breathtaking, proclaiming it to be 'suffocating'.

In 1564 Tintoretto won a competition to decorate the interior, and for the next 23 years much of his time was spent painting the 65 pictures here. The artist began upstairs in the sumptuous **Sala dell'Albergo**, just off the main hall, so make your way straight there before coming back down to the lower hall. On the ceiling is Tintoretto's *The Glory of St Roch*, which was the work that won him the commission. His monumental *Crucifixion* in the same room is said to have been considered by the artist to be his greatest painting.

In the dimly lit main hall, the gilded **ceiling** is covered with 21 immense pictures, and there are another 13 on the walls (all of which are captioned on the helpful plan provided free at the entrance). The best way of studying the ceiling works is to focus on the detail, rather than attempting to take in broad sweeps at once. Hidden in the gloom below the murals are some wonderful, if slightly odd, wooden figures by Venice's off-beat 17th-century sculptor Francesco Pianto.

In contrast to the pictures in the main hall, those on the ground floor (representing scenes from the life of the Virgin) seem almost playful. Look out for *The Flight into Egypt,* widely acknowledged as another of Tintoretto's great paintings. More Tintorettos are on display in the church of San Rocco next door.

CASA DI CARLO GOLDONI

Close to Campo San Polo and the Frari is the **Casa di Carlo Goldoni** (www. visitmuve.it; closed Wed; charge), the house in which the playwright Carlo Goldoni was born in 1707. In 1952 the house was turned into a small museum dedicated to the writer and his works, and although the contents are quite special- ist, the house is worth a visit for its well-preserved Gothic architecture, especially its handsome courtyard.

FONDACO DEI TURCHI

The main route north from Campo di San Polo brings

Tintoretto's 'The Glory of St Roch', Scuola Grande di San Rocco

you into the large, rambling Campo San Giacomo dell'Orio. From here follow the Calle Larga and Fondamenta del Megio for the **Fondaco dei Turchi ⑲**, built in 1227 as a warehouse and meeting place for merchants, but now home to the **Museo di Storia Naturale** (Natural History Museum; www.visitmuve.it; closed Mon; charge). This is a rather old-fashioned collection, but still popular with children.

Among the more terrifying exhibits are a monster crab with legs 2m (6.5ft) long and a scorpion over 30cm (1ft) long. The most impressive exhibits, however, are in the dinosaur room, notably the bones of possibly the largest extinct crocodilian creatures ever found (11m/37ft in length) and the complete skeleton of a massive biped reptile known as an *ouranosaurus* (almost 3.5m/12ft high and some 7m/23ft long).

Venetian gondola outside the Fondaco dei Turchi

CA' PESARO

Zigzag your way east for the next museum on the Grand Canal, the **Galleria Internazionale d'Arte Moderna**, beyond the San Stae landing stage (www.visitmuve.it; closed Mon; charge), housed in the baroque **Ca' Pesaro** ⑳. The gallery was founded with the best of the Biennale exhibition pieces and features mainly Italian artists, with a few important international contemporary works.

Glass figures in Ca' Pesaro, the Galleria Internazionale d'Arte Moderna

In the same building is the **Museo d'Arte Orientale** and the **Galleria Internazionale d'Arte Moderna** (combined ticket), a rather confusing jumble of lacquered pieces, Samurai arms and armour and other artefacts given to Venice by Austria after World War I as reparation for bombing attacks on the city.

CANNAREGIO

HIGHLIGHTS

» The Ghetto, see page 78
» Madonna dell'Orto, see page 80
» Ca' d'Oro, see page 80

This district, close to the railway station, is the most northerly one in Venice. Its name comes from *canne*, meaning reeds, indicating

The Jewish quarter, also known as the Venetian Ghetto

its marshy origins. This is an ancient quarter, often scorned by the snobbish in favour of the more stylish Dorsoduro – ironically, this was once a fashionable spot, dotted with foreign embassies and palatial gardens. The palaces may be faded, but Cannaregio remains both a retreat for cognoscenti and the last bastion for working-class Venetians who have not moved to the Mestre mainland. It is also the site of the world's first Jewish ghetto.

THE GHETTO

For almost 300 years, until Napoleon ended the practice in 1797, the Jews of Venice were permitted to live only in this tiny section of Cannaregio, surrounded on all sides by canals. The area had previously been a foundry or *ghetto* in Venetian; the word *'ghetto'* subsequently came to denote Jewish and other segregated quarters all over the world.

In search of safety and security, Jewish refugees fleeing the War of Cambrai in 1508 came in their thousands to settle here. At the Ghetto's peak in the 17th century, its inhabitants numbered some 5,000, and the limited space led to the building of tenements six storeys high (still tall for Venice).

Venetian Jews were severely taxed, forced to wear distinctive clothing, barred from many professions and made to observe a curfew, which was strictly enforced by watchmen.

However, by the 16th century, the Ghetto was flourishing, with choirs and literary salons that were visited by non-Jewish Venetians. The market at the Campo del Ghetto was the lively 'pawnshop of Venice' – an international attraction where treasures from the great houses of Venice's recently bankrupt or dead were bought and sold.

Today, the Ghetto is a quiet residential corner of Venice, with only a small Jewish population, though the area is rich in Jewish culture with restaurants, bakeries and shops selling Jewish handicrafts. The revamped and expanded **Museo Ebraico** ㉑ (Jewish Museum; www. ghettovenezia.com; closed Sat; charge) located in the Campo del Ghetto Nuovo, contains a remarkable collection of Italian Judaica and runs English-speaking tours of synagogues in the area every hour during opening hours. On the opposite side of the square, a series

Fondamenta Madonna dell'Orto

of reliefs commemorates the 202 Venetian Jews who died in World War II.

MADONNA DELL'ORTO

The 15th-century church of the **Madonna dell'Orto** ㉒ (Our Lady of the Garden; charge) occupies a quiet spot northeast of the Ghetto. After crossing the canal north of the Campo di Ghetto Nuovo, follow the bank east before turning left onto Calle Larga and continuing north through the Campo dei Mori.

The church, which has a delicate Gothic facade and lovely cloister, was built to house a miraculous statue of the Virgin and Child, found in a nearby garden *(orto)*. However, it is best known nowadays for its connections with the Renaissance painter Tintoretto – this was his parish church, and he is buried with his family to the right of the choir, near the high altar.

The church is filled with Tintoretto's paintings, including his *Last Judgement*, *The Worship of the Golden Calf* and *the Presentation of the Virgin* (over the sacristy door), which demonstrates the artist's theatricality and grandiosity. Also of interest is Cima da Conegliano's remarkable painting of *St John the Baptist*, to the right of the entrance.

CA' D'ORO

Head south from the Madonna dell'Orto towards the Strada Nova, which leads east to the **Ca' d'Oro** ㉓, the finest Venetian Gothic palace in the city, which is best viewed from the Grand Canal. Inside is the **Galleria Franchetti** (www.cadoro.org; closed Mon; charge), home to Mantegna's gruesome *St Sebastian*, depicting the saint riddled with arrows, some notable Renaissance sculpture, minor paintings by Tintoretto and Titian, and remnants of frescoes recovered from other buildings, including some by Giorgione.

BOAT TRIP ALONG THE GRAND CANAL

HIGHLIGHTS

The extraordinary main artery through Venice, the **Grand Canal** (Canal Grande) – or *Canalazzo*, as it is known to the locals – stretches over 4km (2 miles), from inauspicious beginnings near the Stazione Ferrovia (railway station) to a glorious final outpouring

The ornate details of a Venetian gondola

into the Basino di San Marco (St Mark's Basin). The views along the canal are so wonderful that many visitors ride the *vaporetti* back and forth for hours, soaking up the atmosphere; a good waterbus to take is the inappropriately named *accelerato* (No. 1), which stops at every landing stage.

The banks of the canal are lined with more than 200 ornate palaces and grand houses, most built between the 14th and 18th centuries. While some have been superbly restored, others have a neglected air, awaiting their turn for renovation. Very few of these homes are still inhabited by the aristocratic families for whom they were built; the majority have been turned into offices, hotels, apartments or gallery spaces.

The following section details some of the most outstanding palaces to look for while travelling along the canal from the railway station (Stazione Ferrovia) towards Piazza San Marco.

FONDACO DEI TURCHI TO THE CA' D'ORO

The first building of note on the right bank is the **Fondaco dei Turchi**, which is home to the Natural History Museum. Built in Veneto-Byzantine style in 1227 (though brutally restored in the 19th century), it is one of the Grand Canal's oldest survivors, once a trading base and living quarters for Turkish merchants.

Just beyond the San Marcuola landing stage on the left bank is the **Palazzo Vendramin-Calergi** (www. casinovenezia.it), designed by Mauro Coducci (1440–1504). The building now provides an opulent setting for Venice's venerable casino. The German composer Richard Wagner died here in 1883 and his apartments on the mezzanine floor are open to visitors (booking required; arwv@ libero.it).

Beyond the San Stae stop on the right bank is the vast baroque **Ca' Pesaro**, designed by Baldassare

The magnificent facade of the Ca' d'Oro

Longhena (the architect of the Salute). Decorated with grotesque masks, the Ca' (short for *Casa*, or house) was completed in 1682 and is now home to two art museums.

By the next landing stage is the **Ca' d'Oro** (home to the Galleria Franchetti), built in the first quarter of the 15th century for the wealthy patrician Marino Contarini. The Ca' was originally covered in gold leaf, hence its name, which means 'House of Gold'. It is one of the most famous frontages on the Grand Canal, renowned for its elaborate Gothic facade decorated with magnificent tracery.

PAST THE RIALTO

Just north of the Rialto, on the left bank, stands the 13th-century Veneto-Byzantine-style **Ca' da Mosto**, one of the oldest houses on

View along the Grand Canal

the canal and, since 2022, home to the sumptuous Venice Venice Hotel. Nearby is the landmark **Ponte di Rialto** (Rialto Bridge). Also on the left bank, to the south, are the handsome twin 13th-century *palazzi* **Loredan** and **Farsetti**, which now function as the town hall. After the San Silvestro stop, on the right bank is the splendid mid-13th century **Palazzo Bernardo**, which may look familiar, since its tracery mirrors that of the Palazzo Ducale.

AROUND THE BEND

Opposite the San Tomà stop is the **Palazzo Mocenigo** complex (www.visitmuve.it; closed Mon; charge), marked by blue-and-white mooring posts *(pali)* and *housing a museum of historical costumes*. The poet Lord Byron lived here from 1819 to 1824, while balancing the needs of a number of fiery local mistresses and working on his mock-heroic narrative poem *Don Juan*. Byron's most daring Venetian venture was to swim in a race against two other men from the Lido all the way to the Rialto – an excellent swimmer, the poet was the only one to finish. Today, the Grand Canal is no longer clean enough for such aquatic feats.

On the bend of the canal, on the opposite side, look out for three attractive palaces: the **Balbi** (1590), the restored **Ca' Foscari** (1437), home to the university, and finally the **Giustinian** (c.1452), where Wagner composed part of his opera *Tristan and Isolde*.

Located a few blocks on is the glorious 17th-century **Ca' Rezzonico**, home to the Museo del Settecento Veneziano. Opposite is the 18th-century **Palazzo Grassi** (www.palazzograssi. it; closed Tues; charge) which belongs to the French magnate, François Pinault, and houses his magnificent collection of contemporary art, as does the Punta della Dogana. The palace can only accommodate a fraction of the vast collection; it is also used as a venue for blockbuster art exhibitions.

PONTE DELL'ACCADEMIA TO LA SALUTE

A little further on is the city's second busiest bridge, the **Ponte dell'Accademia** (Accademia Bridge). Built as a temporary wooden arch in 1932, it replaced an iron structure erected by the Austrians that had become an obstruction to larger *vaporetti*. Restored in 2018, the bridge offers fine views towards La Salute.

The splendid building to the left, with the classic red-and-white *pali*, is the 15th-century **Palazzo Cavalli Franchetti**, while the neighbouring **Palazzo Barbaro**, built from the 15th to the 17th centuries, was much favoured by the artistic and literary set – writers Robert Browning and Henry James, and artists John Singer Sargent, Claude Monet and James Whistler all spent time here.

Next en route is the right bank's **Palazzo Barbarigo**, decorated with strikingly gaudy, late-19th-century mosaics. Close by, the one-storey **Palazzo Venier dei Leoni** is home to the Collezione

Peggy Guggenheim. The final building to note as you head along the canal towards its mouth is the gently listing 15th-century **Ca' Dario** (or Palazzo Dario). Five centuries of scandal, from suicides to bankruptcy to suspicious deaths, have plagued the house. Note its funnel-shaped chimney pots, designed to reduce the risk of fire.

THE ISLANDS

HIGHLIGHTS

A highlight of any visit to Venice is a *vaporetto* trip through the inviting lagoon. Although many of its small islands are uninhabited wildernesses, inaccessible by public transport, there is a range of others to visit, from glass-making Murano to colourful Burano and serene Torcello. For Giudecca, see page 66.

SAN GIORGIO MAGGIORE

San Giorgio Maggiore ㉔ is the closest island to the city, located almost within swimming distance of the Palazzo Ducale. The only major island that is untouched by commerce, it is home to a magnificent Palladian monastic complex and is celebrated for glorious views back over the lagoon towards Venice. To reach the island, take the No. 2 *vaporetto*; the journey lasts little more than five minutes.

Palladio's church (www.abbaziasangiorgio.it; free) was completed in 1610, and the result is a masterpiece of proportion and harmonious space. Tintoretto's *Last Supper* and *The Gathering of Manna* (both 1592–4) grace either side of the chancel. The high altar is dominated by a large bronze group by Girolamo Campagna and represents the evangelists sustaining the world. Behind are the church's splendidly carved 16th-century choir stalls.

San Giorgio Maggiore

For most visitors, however, the church takes second place to the view from its 200-year-old **campanile** (charge). Take the lift to the top for one of the great panoramas of Venice, then look down into the cloister of the **monastery** below to see a rare grassy space. The Fondazione Cini (www.visitcini.it) occupies much of the monastic complex, offering daily guided tours of the verdant grounds. Among various architectural delights, these tours cover the ten so-called 'Vatican Chapels', built for 2018's Bienniale; and the Borges Labyrinth: a twisting, kilometre-long pathway inspired by Argentinian author Jorge Luis Borges, opened in 2021.

SAN MICHELE

The island of **San Michele** ㉕ is the site of the city's cemetery, hence its sombre nickname, the 'island of the dead'. It lies 400m/yds from Fondamenta Nuove and is accessed by *vaporetti* Nos 4.1 and 4.2, which stop right outside **San Michele in Isola**, an elegant Renaissance church clad in glistening white Istrian stone.

┌─ **REST IN PEACE?** ─────────────────────────────

Nowhere is Venice's chronic lack of available land brought home
so vividly as on the cemetery island of San Michele. In the early
1800s Napoleon decreed that burials should no longer take place
in the city, and on San Michele they are not so much welcomed
as tolerated. Burial lasts for 10 years only, however, and unless the
deceased has made provision for an extension on his or her lease
– something that few Venetians can afford – then at the end of
that time the remains are exhumed and sent to an ossuary to
make way for the next occupant.

└──

Go through the cloister to reach the **cemetery** (free). Among the
cypress trees, you can visit the graves of American poet Ezra Pound
(1885–1972), in section XV, and composer Igor Stravinsky (1882–
1971) and impresario Serge Diaghilev (1872–1929), in section XIV.

MURANO

After San Michele, the *vaporetti* stop at **Murano** 🕖, an island
famed for its glassblowing tradition. Free water taxi excursions
are offered by glass factories, but if you want to avoid high-
pressure sales tactics, take the *vaporetto* and make your own way
around the factories instead. Orientation in Murano is a simple
matter. From the main quay, where you disembark at the Colonna
vaporetto stop, stroll along the picturesque Fondamenta dei Vetrai,
which leads to Murano's very own Grand Canal.

Although glass was manufactured in Venice as far back as the
10th century, the open furnaces presented such a fire hazard that
c.1292 the Republic ordered the factories to be transferred to
Murano. Grouped here, the glassblowers kept the secrets of their
trade for centuries; the manufacture of mirrors, for instance, was
for a long time exclusive to Venice.

The island prospered, and by the early 16th century its population reached some 30,000. Glass artisans were considered honoured

citizens. Murano's crystalware decorated royal palaces abroad, and its sumptuous villas housed the leading nobles and diplomats of the city. In time, as other countries learned and applied the secrets of Murano's glassmaking, the island's importance declined, and by the 19th century most of its grand summer residences were no more. However, the glass industry was revived later that century and continues today, though not always up to the old standards and often at over-inflated prices. Still, a number of contemporary glass workshops continue to create outstanding designs.

Signs indicate the **Museo del Vetro** (Glass Museum, Fondamenta Giustinian 8; www.visitmuve.it; charge), containing an eclectic collection of Venetian glass in a 15th-century palazzo. Nearby, on Campo San Donato, is the church of **Santi Maria e**

Contemporary Murano glass

NOTES

It is thought that the Mu-
ranesi were the first to invent
spectacles, in the early 14th
century. By that time, they
were renowned for their win-
dowpanes, which were the
largest and clearest in Europe.

Donato (www.sandonato
murano.it; free), which is
possibly the oldest church
in Venice – its 7th-century
foundations may predate
the Basilica di San Marco. The
church is splendidly atmospheric, and both the brightly
coloured 12th-century
mosaic floor and a golden
mosaic of the Madonna over the high altar have been sympatheti-
cally restored. While you're in the church, note the giant bones
behind the altar; these are said to be those of a dragon slain by
St Donato. Unlike St George, Donato eschewed the conventional
lance and sword, slaying the beast simply by spitting at it.

BURANO

The No. 12 *vaporetto* to **Burano** ㉗ leaves approximately every half
hour from Venice's Fondamenta Nuove; those visiting from Murano
can get the ferry at the Faro (lighthouse) stop. The journey to Burano
and the neighbouring island of Torcello takes around 45 minutes.

Burano is a splash of colour in a bleak lagoon, dispelling any
mournfulness with its parade of colourful fishermen's cottages and
bobbing boats. Naturally hospitable, the islanders are increasingly
known for their "slow food" inns rather than for their lacemaking
and fishing traditions.

The island once produced the world's finest lace, and its exquisitely light *punto in aria* pattern was the most sought after in Europe.
Nowadays, the lace you see in local shops is largely imported from
Asia. But to see authentic Burano lace and the ladies who make it,
visit the **Museo del Merletto** (Lace Museum; Piazza Galuppi; www.
visitmuve.it; closed Mon; charge). Here priceless antique pieces are
displayed behind glass, and you can see the Buranesi hunched over

their handiwork, valiantly keeping the tradition alive. The school was opened in 1872 to retrain the island's women at a time when the numbers of skilled lacemakers had dwindled to just one.

Before leaving the square, visit the 16th-century church of **San Martino** (free), famous for its 18th-century leaning campanile. San Martino is also home to Tiepolo's *Crucifixion*. Just to the north of here is Da Romano (Via Galuppi 221; www.daromano.it; closed Tues) a hearty fish restaurant that is an art attraction in its own right, its walls are filled with numerous paintings.

SAN FRANCESCO DEL DESERTO

From Burano, the peaceful island of **San Francesco del Deserto** makes a lovely detour. The trip takes about 20 minutes and can

Burano waterfront

normally be arranged with a boatman on Burano's main square. St Francis is said to have landed on the island in 1220, on his return from the Holy Land, and Franciscan friars have been here almost ever since. A handful of the brethren choose to make this a permanent home, while young novices spend a year here as part of their training. The monastery (www.sanfrancescodeldeserto.it; closed Mon; donation) has beautiful 14th-century cloisters and gardens.

TORCELLO

From Burano it's a mere five-minute hop on the No. 9 *vaporetto* to the remote and evocative island of **Torcello** ㉘. Amazing as it seems now, in early medieval times this overgrown, almost deserted island was the lagoon's principal city, with an estimated population of 20,000. However, with the silting up of its canals into marshes, a consequent outbreak of malaria and then the ascendancy of Venice, there was a mass exodus from the island. Today, there are only about a dozen inhabitants on Torcello.

As you walk from the *vaporetto* stop to the cathedral, the canal is the only familiarly Venetian feature. On Torcello, buildings have given way to trees, fields and thick undergrowth. The novelist George Sand captured the pastoral mood in the 1830s, 'Torcello is a reclaimed wilderness. Through copses of water willow and hibiscus bushes run saltwater streams where petrel and teal delight to stalk.'

The solitary path leads past the ancient **Ponte del Diavolo** to a small square where Torcello's cathedral, the church of Santa Fosca and the Museo di Torcello (Torcello Museum) all stand. The Italian-Byzantine cathedral **Santa Maria dell'Assunta** (charge) was founded in 639, but dates mostly from 1008, and is therefore the oldest monument in the lagoon. Among the cathedral's treasures is its original 7th-century altar and a Roman sarcophagus containing the relics of St Heliodorus, first Bishop of Altinum (where the island's first settlers were originally from).

Also among the cathedral's highlights are its rich **mosaics**, judged by many to be the finest in Italy outside those at Ravenna. A masterpiece of Byzantine design adorns the central apse, carefully restored in 2021: a slender, mysterious *Madonna* bathed in a cloth of gold. At the opposite end of the building, an entire wall is covered by a complex, heavily restored *Last Judgement*, probably begun early in the 12th century. The steep climb up the campanile will reward you with a panoramic view of the lagoon.

Santa Fosca (free), built in the 11th and 12th centuries and harmoniously combining Romanesque and Byzantine elements, has a bare simplicity rarely found in Venetian churches, while the **Museo di Torcello** (https://servizimetropolitani.ve.it; closed Mon; charge) houses a collection salvaged from long-disappeared churches.

Santa Maria dell'Assunta

At the Lido

THE LIDO

The long strip of land, sandwiched between the city of Venice and the waters of the Adriatic, belongs neither to Venice nor the mainland. This reflects the prime function of the **Lido** 🅺 to protect Venice from the engulfing tides. In spirit, it is a place apart, not quite a traditional summer resort nor a residential suburb. After the time warp of historic Venice, the sight of cars, villas and department stores can be disconcerting. Yet there is a touch of unreality about the Lido, hence its frequent role as a film set. In this faded fantasy, neo-Gothic piles vie with Art Nouveau villas and a mock-Moorish castle.

Since the Lido cannot compete with the historical riches of the rest of Venice, it generally remains the preserve of residents and visitors staying on the island. Although most day-trippers stray no further than the smart hotels and the beaches where the poets

Byron and Shelley once raced on horseback, the Lido offers subtle pleasures for those willing to look, from belle époque architecture to a delightful cycle ride along the sea walls to Malamocco.

The ferries from San Marco deposit visitors among the traffic at the edge of the shopping district. Close to the jetties stands the 16th-century church of **Santa Maria Elisabetta**, behind is the main street, Gran Viale Santa Maria Elisabetta, which cuts across the island from the lagoon shore to the Adriatic. At the far end of the Viale lies the **Lungomare**, the scenic seafront promenade. Beyond are the best Adriatic beaches, private pockets of sand bedecked with colourful cabins.

The Lido is home to several of the city's most elegant hotels, even if the palatial **Grand Hôtel des Bains** of *Death in Venice* fame (see box) has been closed for some time, still awaiting a long-promised conversion into a boutique hotel.

DEATH IN VENICE

Death and Venice go together, with the lagoon a familiar backdrop to modern murder mysteries. The city's taste for the macabre is partly a romanticised notion fed by visions of sinister alleys, the inkiness of a lagoon night or a *cortège* of mourning gondolas gliding across the water. However, Venetian history does provide tales of murdered doges and deadly plots nipped in the bud by the secret police.

And the most celebrated work of literature set in Venice, Thomas Mann's novella *Death in Venice*, does little to dispel the myth. The book follows the decline of the writer Gustav von Aschenbach – a man who believes that art is produced only in 'defiant despite' of corrupting passions and physical weakness. On a reluctant break from work, Aschenbach finds himself in Venice, which Mann depicts as a place of decadence and spiritual dislocation. Aschenbach's obsession with a beautiful Polish boy staying at his hotel (the Lido's former Grand Hôtel des Bains) has dire consequences, as he becomes a slave to his passions, ignoring a cholera epidemic that the corrupt Venetian authorities try to conceal.

Murano glass artwork on display

Things to do

It may surprise that Venice – despite being sliced by canals large and small and twisting walkways (*calli*) impassable to cars – is easily navigable on foot. Bridges are plentiful in the historic core while regular *vaporetti* (waterbuses) circle the city and ply the broader gaps between land. Indeed, simply wandering and relishing the vistas around every corner is among the most worthwhile activities here. Most of the main sights are clustered within easy reach on a leisurely stroll.

No matter when you go to Venice there will be waterfront cafés made for lingering, Baroque concerts in grand churches, and tiny *bacari* (wine bars) made for toasting the city over a glass of Prosecco and a plate of seafood tapas. Venice offers year-round concerts, opera, theatre, art exhibitions and festivals ranging from Carnival to water pageants. Take to the water yourself on a gondola ride.

CULTURE

Venetians are passionate about their classical music and proud of the fact that Vivaldi, Monteverdi and Wagner all lived in the city. **Concerts** are staged everywhere, but especially in churches and palaces. Popular venues for concerts, from organ recitals to choral works, are the churches of Santo Stefano, the Frari, San Vidal, the Salute and Castello's Santa Maria della Pietà (www.vivaldichurch. it). The lavishly decorated Scuole, the charitable confraternities, also stage regular concerts. Baroque music predominates, with the works of former Venice resident Antonio Vivaldi particularly celebrated. The chamber group **Interpreti Veneziani** (www.interpretiveneziani.com) is a good name to look out for – they perform on 18th-century instruments in Chiesa San Vidal (Accademia *vaporetto* stop). Other more operatic ensembles include **Musica a Palazzo** (www.musicapalazzo.com) who perform in the Palazzo

Barbarigo-Minotto along the Grand Canal, where you can listen to arias by Verdi and Rossini ring out under a Tiepolo-frescoed ceiling.

For **opera performances**, the premier venue is **La Fenice** (The Phoenix), once dubbed 'the prettiest theatre in Europe'. Badly damaged by fire in 1996 (its third fire since its construction in 1774), it reopened in 2004. The opera season runs from November until May (book through http://teatrolafenice.it or www.veneziaunica.it).

Art flows through the veins of Venice, with **Gallerie dell'Accademia** among many other prestigious galleries satisfying the eclectic tastes of the world of **visual art**. The Accademia is a treasury of Venetian art ranging from Renaissance masterpieces and Byzantine panels to ceremonial paintings, but it is as memorable for its snapshots of everyday life as for its sumptuous

George and Amal Clooney at Venice Film Festival in 2017

showpieces. Meanwhile, modern art collections, especially the **Peggy Guggenheim Collection** and **Ca' Pesaro**, give Venice a formidable platform from which to sell itself as a truly modern art hub.

Don't miss the Guggenheim and Punta della Dogana masterpieces by Bellini, Titian and Tintoretto. Churches and *scuole* (lay confraternities) are repositories of glowing treasures from the Venetian school; for the very best under one roof, head to the Accademia gallery in Dorsoduro. Art lovers should concentrate on the *Quadreria*, inconspicuously located in rather gloomy rooms on the second floor of the **Correr Museum**; a fine collection of Venetian Renaissance works includes a room of pieces by the Bellinis and the famous Carpaccio painting, *Two Venetian Noblewomen*.

FESTIVALS

As a major event on the international cinema circuit, the ten-day **Venice Film Festival** opened in 1932, predating Cannes by 14 years. Founded as a showcase for Fascist Italy, the festival's success belies its unpromising origins. In balmy late August–early September, Venice welcomes the stars, who can be seen parading along the Lido seafront or sipping Bellinis near St Mark's. To attend, check www.labiennale.org.

Among other landmark festivals in Venice is a raft of historic masquerade parades and pageants. These are the glory of Venice, with palaces on the Grand Canal festooned with streamers and silks, redolent of the pomp and pageantry of the Republic. Best known is the pre-Lenten **Carnival**, packing the *campi* tight for storied balls. Some of the largest of Venice's celebrations spill over into the water, such as April's **Festa di San Marco** (St Mark's Day), featuring a gondola race; May's **La Sensa**, honouring Venice's marriage with the sea; and September's **La Regatta Storica** (www. regatastoricavenezia.it), the year's premier rowing event.

THE COCKTAIL HOUR

Between 6pm and 8pm is 'cocktail time', a Venetian ritual. The locals can be seen sipping wine or classic cocktails in both chic cafés and old-fashioned neighbourhood *bacari*. To look like a Venetian, try the lurid orange cocktail known as *spritz* (pronounced 'spriss' in Venetian dialect). The bright-orange drink was introduced under Austrian rule (named after the introduction of 'selzer', fizzy soda water) and soon became a firm favourite. It consists of roughly equal parts of Prosecco, soda water and Campari or Aperol, garnished with a twist of lemon or an olive. Ask for a *spritz al bitter* for a stronger, less cloying taste. The *spritz* can be an acquired taste, but once acquired, it's the clearest sign that you've fallen for Venice.

NIGHTLIFE

A conservative spirit and an ageing population mean that sleepy Venetian nightlife plays on romance, intimacy and charm rather than cutting-edge clubs and urban thrills. For smart nightlife, call into the cocktail bars in the historic hotels and lap up the stylish San Marco haunts. At the less formal end of the scale, don't leave without popping into one of the city's traditional wine bars, known as *bacari*. Having *cichetti e l'ombra*, a snack and a glass of wine, is a Venetian tradition, similar to Spanish tapas.

The best spot to embark on a *giro di ombra* (bar crawl) is the Rialto, the mercantile heart of Venice. Here, the canalside **Erberia** area has become a popular meeting place at cocktail hour. These bars tend to be new-wave *bacari* (wine bars) that look traditional but have dared to redesign the menu in tune with the times. In summer the nightlife scene switches to the **Venice Lido**, focusing on the seafront and the grand hotels. You may also find yourself rubbing shoulders with the glitzy set, especially during the film festival. Just beyond San Marco are serious wine bars (*enoteche*), where tastings are the main draw.

SHOPPING

WHERE TO SHOP

Venice is divided into six *sestieri* (districts) with very different characters. The most elegant boutiques are on Calle Vallaresso, Salizada San Moisè, the Frezzeria and Calle Larga XXII Marzo, west of San Marco. But far more fun is the classic fabric and haberdashery quarter known as Le Mercerie, a maze of alleys that winds between San Marco and the Rialto. Bevilacqua has been making and selling its Tessitura Luigi Bevilacqua collection of velvets, lampasses, damasks and brocades since the late 19th century. Between San Marco and the Rialto are shops selling marbled paper; Murano glass can be found here, too. San Polo and Santa Croce are adjoining districts that

Luxury shopping in Dolce & Gabbana

encompass the labyrinthine Rialto market, the commercial heart of the lagoon. Just off Campo Santa Maria Formosa – a city square in the Castello district – is the authentic mask shop, Papier Mâché.

WHAT TO BUY

The full range of Italian designer goods are on sale in Venice. But above all, seek out traditional Venetian crafts for a secret glimpse of Venetians at their best. Among the most in-demand items are elegant, personalized stationery, hand-crafted ceramics (most famously Murano glass), hand-tooled, leatherbound notebooks, and variously bedazzled Carnival masks. Buy them at **Papier Mâché** (Calle Lunga Santa Maria Formosa, Castello 5174), run by Stefano Gottardo, a man much to thank for the tradition's revival;

Carnival mask maker

CARNEVALE

The black cloak, tricorn hat, white mask and other rather sinister garb identified with Venice's Carnevale date back to the 18th century when the *commedia dell'arte* was in vogue. In the final century of the decadent, drifting Republic, Carnevale was extended to six months, and Venetians wore these costumes from December to June. Under this guise of anonymity, commoner and aristocrat were interchangeable, husbands and wives could pursue illicit love affairs. Things got so out of hand that Carnevale was eventually banned.

Today's Carnevale, revived only in 1979 and held in February/March, is more restrained. Nonetheless, this is one time of year that the city really comes to life, with street parties, masked balls, pageants, special events and visitors from all over Europe.

or rent a stunning Carnival disguise at Atelier Nicolao (Cannaregio 2590; www.nicolao.com) to slip back into Casanova's era.

GLASSWARE

It's fashionable to mock Murano glass, but the best pieces are works of art, from show-stopping chandeliers to sophisticated sculptures signed by great Italian artists and designers. The illustrious names include Barovier & Toso (Fondamenta Vetrai 28, Murano, www.barovier.com/en) and **Venini** (Piazzetta dei Leoncini, San Marco, www.venini.com). Board a *vaporetto* to the island's official **Murano Glass Museum** (Museo del Vetro; https://museovetro.visitmuve.it), its collection spanning back to 15th-century works, or cross the water from St Mark's Square to **Le Stanze del Vetro** (https://lestanzedelvetro.org; free), a sleek museum on the monastic island of San Giorgio. Running in partnership with the Fondazione Cini, the museum is dedicated to 20th-century and contemporary glass. At the south end of Murano, you can also catch local masters in action in Murano's **Glass Cathedral** (www.santachiaramurano.com).

OUTDOOR ACTIVITIES

At the end of October, the city hosts a world-class **marathon**; to participate, visit https://venicemarathon.it.

Families might prefer a summer trip to the Lido, either cycling or lapping up the private beaches. Watersports on offer include **windsurfing**, **water-skiing** and **canoeing**, or **dinghy** and **catamaran sailing**. However, swimming is not always permitted on the Lido's beaches due to pollution problems.

Knowledge of the lagoon's channels is necessary for safe boating, but you can still do a **skippered cruise** or hire a boat. If, instead, you wish to try your hand at **Venetian rowing**, even for a couple of hours, contact Row Venice (www.rowvenice.com). For **kayaking** in the Venetian backwaters or exploring the wilds of

Fireworks at Festa del Redentore

the lagoon, Venice Kayak offers supervised kayak tours, even for children (aged eight and up; www.venicekayak.com).

VENICE FOR CHILDREN

The waterways of Venice never fail to impress the young at heart, making a gondola ride a good choice for family entertainment. Alternatively, simply take the kids on a *vaporetto* – Venice's water-buses offer the distinct advantage that children under four years of age travel free, and there are reduced fares for families. Excursions to the Lido, where there are beaches, water rides and pedalos, are always popular with children.

Other child-friendly options include: watching the glass-blowers at **Murano**; visiting the **Museo Storico Navale**, with its fascinating array of life-size ships; climbing up the **Campanile di San Marco**; making their own Carnival masks (Dorsoduro; www.camacana.com). Finally, consider a July trip to see the **Festa del Redentore** with its fabulous fireworks display (see Festivals and events).

FESTIVALS AND EVENTS

1 Jan *Capodanno* (New Year's Day). Beachfront celebrations.
Feb–Mar *Carnevale* (Carnival). Ten-day, pre-Lenten extravaganza with masked balls, processions, pantomime and music. The high point comes on Shrove Tuesday with a masked ball in Piazza San Marco, after which the effigy of Carnival is burned in the square.
25 Apr *Festa di San Marco* (St Mark's Day). Ceremonial Mass in the Basilica, when rosebuds *(bocoli)* are given as love tokens. A gondola race is also held between Sant'Elena and the Punta della Dogana, followed by a traditional soup of *risi e bisi* ('rice and peas').
Sunday after Ascension *La Sensa*. Celebrating Venice's 'marriage with the sea'. Re-enacts trips made to the Lido by the doges, who cast rings into the water to symbolise the union of the Republic and the sea.

La Biennale di Venezia

Two Sundays after Ascension *La Vogalonga* (literally: 'long row'). Hundreds of rowing boats follow a 32km (20-mile) course from the Basino di San Marco to Burano and then San Francesco del Deserto.

June–Aug *Venezia Jazz Festival*. Welcoming an international lineup.

June–Nov *Biennale dell'Arte* (even years only). Art exhibition held in the Arsenale and Giardini Pubblici. *Biennale Architettura* (odd years only). Architecture exhibition in the same spaces.

July, third Sunday *Festa del Redentore* (Festival of the Redeemer). A sweeping bridge of boats bedecked in finery and glowing with lights stretches across the Giudecca Canal to Il Redentore church. There is a spectacular firework display on the eve of the feast day.

Aug/Sept Venice hosts the International Film Festival at the Lido by day, San Marco by night.

15 Aug *Ferragosto* (Assumption). Concerts on Torcello.

Sept, first Sunday *La Regata Storica* (Historical Regatta). The finest regatta of the year, which begins with a procession up the Grand Canal led by costumed Venetians, followed by gondola races.

Nov–May Opera season at La Fenice.

21 Nov *Festa della Salute*. Processions to the candlelit Santa Maria della Salute, commemorating the city's deliverance from the plague of 1630.

Food and drink

As the hub of a cosmopolitan trading empire, Venice was bristling with multicultural communities, each with a distinctive culinary heritage. While remaining rooted in rich tradition today, its restaurants have enjoyed a renaissance of late, with creative takes on old favourites and a sharpened eye for sustainable, locally-sourced food, seasonal menus and an expanding selection of natural wines. Partially due to the difficulty of transporting and stocking supplies, prices are relatively high. But dining on a budget is itself supported by a long-time, popular tradition: namely, *cicchetti*: cheap tapas-style snacks to accompany a glass of wine or an Aperol spritz, another Veneto original.

TOP 10 THINGS TO TRY

1. CICCHETTI

Enjoying *cicchetti* (Venetian tapas) and fine wines by the glass in the city's traditional *bacari* (taverns) is almost a rite of passage for foodies. Venetian *bacari* invariably offer a selection of plates on their counters, from *polpette* (spicy meatballs) to *carciofini* (artichoke hearts); *seppie rose* (grilled cuttlefish); anchovy nibbles; *francobolli* (crustless 'postage stamp' sandwiches); slivers of dried salt cod; *baccalà mantecato*

Venetian tapas

The infamous italian gelato

(creamy salt cod); *sarde in saor* (marinated sardines); to cured meats and crostini with grilled vegetables. Many of the best *bacari* are those clustered in and around the Rialto. It's always worth asking what specials (*piatti del giorno*) are on offer; these are often the freshest and most creative dishes. Along with your *cicchetti*, enjoy an *ombra* (glass of wine).

2. SEAFOOD

Venetian food is heavily influenced by the bounty of the lagoon, with fresh fish, clams, shrimps, calamari, *seppie* (cuttlefish) and octopus all featuring heavily. You'll also find plenty of cod, 'tenderised' for the great *baccalà mantecato* (cream of dried cod) and *grancevole* – red Adriatic spider crab. Most Venetian fish dishes come from the Adriatic, but inland fishing also occurs in *valli*, fish farms in the lagoon, mainly for grey mullet (*cefalu*) and eel (*anguilla*). It's hard to better *antipasti di frutti di mare*, a feast of simply cooked shellfish and molluscs, prawns and soft-shelled crabs vying with baby octopus and squid, drizzled with olive oil and lemon juice. A trademark dish is cuttlefish risotto, served black and pungent with cuttlefish ink. *Tartuffi di mare* (sea truffles) are also popular, as are mussels pan-fried with parsley and garlic (*peoci saltati*), salt cod (*baccalà*) and spider crab, boiled and then dressed simply in lemon and oil (*granseola*).

3. APERITIVO

In Venice, local Veneto wines predominate, from sparkling Prosecco, the perfect *aperitif*, to crisp Soave, fruity, garnet-red Bardolino and the less prestigious Valpolicella. Venetians drink far more white wine than red, partly because it is a better accompaniment to seafood.

The Bellini, a combination of Prosecco and fresh peach juice, was supposedly invented in *Harry's Bar*, still a stylish spot for cocktails near San Marco. The other classic local cocktail is spritz, an orangey concoction made of Campari or bitters, white wine and soda water. To widen your wine knowledge, look out for an *enoteca*, a combination of wine bar and wine merchant, a cosy spot that probably also serves snacks.

Restaurant Terrazza Danieli

4. FEGATO ALLA VENEZIANA

Fish may reign superior in Venice, but offal is also popular, particularly when used in *fegato alla veneziana* – calf's liver sliced and pan-fried with parsley and onions. Although now found all over the country, the dish is a Venetian speciality. Besides creamy polenta, this rich, wholesome dish is also commonly served with fresh bread or *risi e bisi* (Italian rice and peas).

5. RISOTTO

Ever since its introduction to Venice by Arab communities, *riso* (rice) has punted pasta into second place, and risotto is a classic Venetian dish, often made with seafood or seasonal vegetables. *Risi e bisi* (rice and peas) is a thick soup blended with ham, celery and onion. Equally delicious are the seasonal risottos, cooked with asparagus tips, artichoke hearts, fennel, courgettes or pumpkins. Another variant involves sultanas and pine nuts. A trademark dish is cuttlefish risotto, served black and pungent with ink, or *granseola*, spider crab, boiled and then dressed simply in lemon and oil.

6. CREMA FRITTA ALLA VENEZIANA

The Venetians introduced sugar cane to the rest of Europe and have retained their sweet tooth. An especially sugary dessert is *crema fritta alla veneziana*, a fried custard dessert often found on the menu at Christmas or during Carnival. It can be eaten hot or cold and is traditionally served with a glass of raisin wine. Once fried, this dessert is dusted in sugar and sliced into bite-size pieces. Its golden, crunchy exterior provides a nice contrast to its soft and pillowy centre.

7. CHEESE

Blessed are the dairy counters of Venice when it comes to cheese: laden with diversely assorted piquant offerings from across the Veneto region. Of these, Asiago is among the most celebrated. This protected cow's milk cheese, produced on the Asiago plateau in the

Tiramisu, the quintessential Italian dessert

Veneto foothills, assumes different textures, becoming more crumbly with age: from *mezzano* (4–6 months) to *vecchio* (10 months and over) to *stravecchio* (15 months plus). Another regional speciality is Bastardo del Grappa, whose name derives in part from the 'mixed milk' historically used by cheesemakers of the Venetian Prealps to make it. Ubriaco is decadent and undeniably Venetian, doused with Prosecco, giving it a decidedly fruity character.

8. ZAETI

Diamond-shaped *zaeti* biscuits ('the little yellow ones') can be found in supermarkets, bakeries and patisseries across the city. These sweet biscuits are traditionally diamond-shaped but are also sometimes baked in rounds. Though recipes vary among families (and bakeries), the basic ingredients remain the same: polenta flour and raisins. The

Make it a habit to ask what specials *(piatti del giorno)* are on offer. These are often the freshest and most innovative dishes on the menu. Home-made pasta and seasonal offerings based on what's fresh from the market are typical.

recipe was historically used by poor farming families with access to limited ingredients. Locals eat these after a main meal or as a snack during Lent. A popular local way to eat *zaeti* is by dipping them in wine, such as Recioto (a sweet Venetian wine) or Vin Santo.

9. GELATO

Like the rest of Italy, Venice is blessed with first-rate *gelatarie* (ice cream shops). An infinitude of flavours awaits, from hazelnut gianduja to praline to fig and tiramisu. Look for *gelaterie* that make their own ice cream, piling their unusual creations high like multicoloured mountains of temptation. A refreshing alternative is granita, shaved ice, usually with a coffee or fruit flavour.

10. TIRAMISÙ

Comprising this heady epicurean treat are savoiardi biscuits dipped in coffee and marsala (fortified dessert wine), melded with mascarpone, egg yolks and sugar, and dusted with cocoa. Its origins have been linked to nearby Treviso, where, in the 19th century, it was baked using traditional Austrian and Hapsburg recipes. Today it's found all over the country, including in most *pasticcerie* and restaurants in Venice. While recipes vary widely, a generous shot of marsala is usually thrown in to cut through the cream.

WHERE TO EAT

Venetian restaurants range in style from cool, 18th-century elegance – especially in San Marco (St Mark's) and Castello – to rustic gentility. Yet individualistic inns abound, tucked under pergolas or spilling onto terraces and courtyards. More upmarket places are termed **ristoranti**, but may be called **osterie** (inns) if they focus on simple food in an intimate or homely setting.

Steer clear of the tourist traps that dominate major tourist hubs, most notably San Marco. Not that the grandest of the square's restaurants and cafés should be dismissed out of hand: At least for special occasions, Venetians also patronise Harry's Bar, Florian and, not least, Quadri.

Moving away from St Mark's generally sees both the crowds (and the prices) fall away. Look out for *bacari,* traditional Venetian tapas bars, and chic wine bars around the Rialto market, in San Polo and Santa Croce. In addition to a further sprinkling of *bacari*, Cannaregio

A market seller on the San Barnaba Canal

hosts some of the most stylish wine bars in town, while Dorsoduro is stacked with sophisticated cafés, some linked to the area's art galleries. Some of the most enchanting and authentic dining experiences are found even farther afield on Venice's outlying islands, from Giudecca just across the canal to Burano and the adjacent Mazzorbo – home to one of Venice's six Michelin-starred establishments: Venissa (www.venissa.it), a champion of sustainable cooking.

DINE LIKE A LOCAL

Most Venetians start off the day with a coffee and croissant *(cornetto)* in a caffè (usually 7–9am), though most better-quality hotels serve a buffet breakfast, whether continental, English, or American-style.

Spaghetti with clams and mussels

A VENETIAN WINE CRAWL

Bacari are traditional wine bars that also serve a Venetian version of tapas, known as *cicchetti*. A *bacari* crawl, especially in the authentic Rialto or Cannaregio areas, represents one of the highlights of any stay in Venice. When planning a route, be influenced by neighbourhood, mood and personal taste for authenticity, tranquillity or live music. Known as a *giro di ombre*, a bar crawl is best begun at sunset as some of the more traditional bars close early. These time-warp taverns are the perfect introduction to *cicchetti*, from slivers of dried salt cod (*baccala*) slathered on *crostini*, to tiny meatballs or sweet and sour sardines – usually washed down with Prosecco. Other cheap but often sensational tapas include calamari, marinated radicchio, fried mozzarella balls, asparagus tarts, Venetian sushi, or shrimp wrapped in pancetta.

Both lunch (*pranzo*; 12.30–2.30pm) and dinner (*cena*; typically starting no earlier than 7pm) can range from snacks at a *bacaro* to a more substantial, sit-down meal at a *ristorante* or *osteria*: risotto or pasta as the first course (*primo piatto*), often paired with seafood from the lagoon as the *secondo*, often served with bread to help scoop up any leftover sauce from the plate. For the freshest food, steer clear of the tourist traps (give-aways include laminated photos of dishes, discounted 'tourist menus' and callers outside trying to lure you in. Try to adjust to the local time in order to take the best advantage of the menu (go too late, and they may run out of things). Late-night dining can be difficult to find in Venice, so you'll generally need to settle on somewhere by 9pm.

The bill usually includes service (*servizio*) of between 10 and 15 percent but ask if you're not sure. It's normal to round the bill up slightly in addition to this.

Though not confined to a specific mealtime, the *cicchetti* tradition comes alive in the late afternoon and early evening, with tapas-style finger foods eaten alongside an *ombra* (glass of wine).

TO HELP YOU ORDER

Waiter/waitress **Cameriere/cameriera**

Do you have a set menu? **Avete un menù a prezzo fisso?**

I'd like a/an/some … **Vorrei …**

beer **una birra**	pepper **del pepe**
bread **del pane**	potatoes **delle patate**
butter **del burro**	salad **un'insalata**
coffee **un caffè**	salt **del sale**
cream **della panna**	soup **una minestra**
fish **del pesce**	sugar **dello zucchero**
fruit **della frutta**	tea **un tè**
ice cream **un gelato**	water (mineral) **dell'acqua (minerale)**
meat **della carne**	wine **del vino**
milk **del latte**	

MENU READER

aglio garlic	**mela** apple
agnello lamb	**melanzane** aubergine
albicocche apricots	**merluzzo** cod
aragosta lobster	**ostriche** oysters
arancia orange	**pesca** peach
bistecca beefsteak	**pollo** chicken
carciofi artichokes	**pomodori** tomatoes
cipolle onions	**prosciutto** ham
crostacei shellfish	**seppie** cuttlefish
fiche figs	**tacchino** turkey
formaggio cheese	**tonno** tuna
frutti di mare seafood	**uovo** egg
funghi mushrooms	**uva** grapes
lamponi raspberries	**verdure** vegetables
maiale pork	**vitello** veal
manzo beef	**vongole** clams

Places to eat

We have used the following symbols to give an idea of the price for a two-course meal for one, including house wine and service:

€€€€ = over €90

€€€ = €60–90

€€ = €25–60

€ = up to €25

SAN MARCO

RESTAURANTS

Acqua Pazza Campo Sant'Angelo, San Marco 3808, www.veniceacqua-pazza.com. This slick, upmarket restaurant is based on a trendy square, serving Neapolitan pizzas or fine seafood when Venetian squid ink is too exotic to contemplate. Specialities include ricotta-stuffed courgette flowers and spaghetti with clams. A post-coffee Limoncello is on the house. Vaporetto: S. Angelo. €€€

Harry's Bar Calle Vallaresso 1323, San Marco 1323, www.cipriani.com/harrys-bar. The consistency of this legendary bar and restaurant also draws a resolutely Venetian crowd. The unpretentious tone (if not the price) is perfect. Sip a Bellini (Prosecco and peach juice, invented here), even if your budget keeps you from having a second. Vaporetto: San Marco Vallaresso. €€€€

Trattoria Do Forni Calle degli Specchieri, www.doforni.it. An upmarket but old-school spot with rambling yet intimate rooms. What it lacks in views it more than makes up for in atmosphere. The relatively extensive menu embraces Italian classics, offering a variety of traditional pasta dishes along with international and Venetian specialities. Vaporetto: San Marco Giardinetti. €€€

CAFÉS AND BARS

Caffè Florian Piazza San Marco, https://caffeflorian.com. Established in 1720, Caffè Florian, perhaps quite rightly, claims to be the oldest café in Europe. The exquisite interior is just one reason for its popularity in addition to the range of coffees, pastries, cakes and snacks on offer. Also serves wine and cocktails for a classy aperitivo.

Grancaffè Quadri Piazza San Marco, www.alajmo.it/grancaffe-quadri. Founded in 1683, this baroque grand café is a Venetian institution, perfect for people-watching over a wintry hot chocolate and cakes or cocktails and nibbles (Quadri's gourmet restaurant upstairs €€€€). Vaporetto: San Marco Vallaresso.

CASTELLO

RESTAURANTS

Al Covo Campiello della Pescaria, www.ristorantealcovo.com. Covo's fine reputation draws foodies to sample the fish-heavy tasting menu. The moeche (softshell crab) lightly fried with onions vie with Adriatic tuna, or squid-ink pasta with clams and courgette flowers. Booking essential for this formal spot. Vaporetto: Arsenale. €€€

Alle Testiere Calle del Mondo Novo, Castello 5801, www.osterialletestiere. it. Located near Campo Santa Maria Formosa, this renowned seafood restaurant demands booking (few tables). The menu harks back to Venice's days on the spice route; razor clams or pasta may be subtly spiced; fine wine list. Vaporetto: San Zaccaria. €€€

Enoiteca Guesteria La Caneva da Mauro Lorenzon Calle dei Forni 2282/A, www.ostemaurolorenzon.com. Settled into a new location near the Rio dell'Arsenale post-pandemic, this cosy, rustic *bacaro* has been run by an eccentric wine buff host for decades. Nibble on charcuterie at the counter, or opt for the decent-sized, rotating menu. Expect a laid-back jazz atmosphere and superb wines. Vaporetto: Rialto. €€

L'Osteria di Santa Marina Campo Santa Marina 5911, www.osteriadis-antamarina.com. Set in a quiet square, this deceptively simple trattoria presents reinterpretations of Venetian classics, from cuttlefish ink ravioli with sea bass to seafood pasta, fresh turbot, tuna, and beef carpaccio, tuna-and-bean soup and mixed grills. Finish with a palate-cleansing sorbet or comforting cinnamon apple pie. Vaporetto: Rialto. €€€

DORSODURO

RESTAURANTS

Lineadombra Dorsoduro 19, Fondamenta Zattere Ai Saloni, www.ristor-antelineadombra.com. A charming restaurant offering beautiful views of Guidecca Canal and the Palladian churches of Redentore and San Giorgio. Known for using seasonal ingredients to produce traditional Venetian dishes and fresh seafood. €€

Oniga Campo San Barnaba, www.oniga.it. Dine inside or on the campo after opting for the Venetian seafood platter or the vegetarian option. For once, vegetarians can be spoilt with an array of pasta dishes made with artichokes, aubergines and pecorino cheese. *Oniga* takes pride in its use of seasonal, high-quality ingredients. Vaporetto: Ca' Rezzonico. €€

Osteria Ca' del Vento Calle del Vento 1518/A, www.osteriacadelvento.it. This atmospheric family-run restaurant is slightly off the beaten track and serves up traditional Italian fare, all based on fresh local produce. A lot of vegetarian options are available. It's a small restaurant tucked away from the tourist crowds and popular with locals, so it's best to book in advance. Vaporetto: San Basilio. €€

CAFÉS AND BARS

Cantinone del Vino già Schiavi Fondamenta Nani, Rio di San Trovaso, www.cantinaschiavi.com. This old-fashioned canalside wine bar is overly popular with Venetians and visitors from all walks of life. It's standing-room only and an excellent place for grazing on *cicchetti* – among the most inventive in Venice. Savour the mood by propping up the bar over a light lunch or lingering over cocktails. Vaporetto: Zattere.

Gelateria Nico Fondamenta Zattere Al Ponte Lungo, 922, www.gelateri-anico.com. In business since 1937, this longstanding ice cream bar along the Zattere promenade is somewhat of an institution. Choose from 26 flavours of ice cream and enjoy your sweet treat on the terrace overlooking gorgeous views of the water.

SAN POLO AND SANTA CROCE

RESTAURANTS

Alla Madonna Calle della Madonna 594, www.ristoranteallamadonna.com. With a focus on tradition, this arty, bustling, ever-popular trattoria (no reservations) serves meticulously prepared seafood, fresh from the lagoon. Tuck into Sant'Erasmo artichokes or a seafood risotto while also being seduced by the impressive art collection. Vaporetto: Rialto Mercato. €€–€€€

Alla Zucca Ponte del Megio, off Campo San Giacomo dell'Orio, tel: 041 524 1570, www.lazucca.it. This popular trattoria is set by a crooked canal bridge, with a few additional tables outside. The bohemian atmosphere reflects the vegetable-inspired menu (aubergine pasta, smoked ricotta, pumpkin flan) as well as meat and fish. It's a popular alternative to the typical Venetian restaurant. Reservations exclusively by phone. Vaporetto: San Stae. €€

Cantina Do Spade Calle delle Do Spade, Rialto, www.cantinadospade. com. One of the oldest Rialto *bacari* is still going strong. Expect deep-fried calamari, *baccala* (salted cod), meatballs and other typical *cicchetti* (tapas). Stand at the bar and chat to Venetians or grab a table for a traditional meal. The service is prompt and friendly. Vaporetto: Rialto Mercato. €

Da Fiore Calle del Scaleter, 2202/A, just north of Campo di San Polo, www. ristorantedafiore.com. Regularly ranked among the best restaurants in town, this reflects the subtlety of Venetian cuisine, from grilled calamari and *granseola* (spider crab) to Adriatic tuna, squid, sashimi and *risotto al nero di seppia* (cuttlefish risotto). Vaporetto: San Tomà. €€€€

Glam Calle Tron, 1961, Santa Croce, www.enricobartolini.net. Set in a tranquil courtyard of the luxurious Palazzo Venart with a rare frontal view of the Grand Canal, this elegant restaurant bears the distinction of being the only double Michelen-starred restaurant in historic Venice. Young chef Donato Ascani is known for contemporary spins on dishes rooted in Venetian tradition, predominantly sourced from the natural bounty of the lagoon. Vaporetto: San Stae. €€€€

Ristorante Ribot Fondamenta Minotto, Rio del Gaffaro, Santa Croce, tel: 041-524 3126. This authentic neighbourhood restaurant is superb value (try the risotto, grilled scallops or seafood pasta) but also has a secret garden, and live music in the evening. Piazzale Roma (Station). €€

CANNAREGIO

RESTAURANTS

Algiubagio Fondamenta Nuove 5039, www.algiubagio.net. This contemporary *bacaro* is the perfect place for chatting over *cicchetti*, or for waiting for the ferry to Murano, Burano or the airport (via Alilaguna). A good but pricier restaurant attached. Vaporetto: Fondamenta Nuove. €€

Al Vecio Bragosso Strada Nuova, Cannaregio 4386, www.alveciobragosso.com. The family has a fishing *bragozzo* (hence the name), which hauls in fresh seafood each day. Try the Venetian classics *sarde in saor* (sardines in an onion sauce) or *baccalà mantecato* (boiled cod on toast). Vaporetto: Ca' d'Oro. €€

Alla Frasca Cannaregio 5176, tel: 041-241 2585. Hidden in the backstreets, this friendly, genuine inn serves fresh, no-frills local cuisine; dine on grilled fish or spaghetti with clams in the pretty courtyard and finally feel like a Venetian. Vaporetto: Fondamenta Nuove. €

Ca Dolfin Cannaregio 5903, tel: 041-528 5299. This tiny restaurant near the Rialto Bridge is a favourite among local gourmets and tourists alike for authentic Italian food. The sea bass with courgettes and peppers and spaghetti with mussels are really worth a try, just as the rest of the menu. Booking ahead is recommended. Vaporetto: Rialto. €€

Da Rioba Fondamenta della Misericordia, www.darioba.com. This rustic-chic restaurant is set on a canal that comes alive at night, and you can dine outside, by the bustling waterfront. The cooking is subtly creative – whether with pasta dishes or with seafood, including tuna carpaccio. Vaporetto: San Marcuola. €€

Gam Gam Calle Ghetto Vecchio 1123, www.gamgamkosher.com. Set at the entrance to the world's oldest ghetto, this kosher restaurant has served up Sephardic specialties since 1996, run by a family with roots in Jewish Venice that trace back to the 15th century. An affordable menu includes cous cous, latkes, schnitzel, moussaka and matza ball soup. Vaporetto: Guglie. €€

Vini da Gigio Calle Stua Cannaregio 3628A, www.vinidagigio.com. Both cosy and romantic, this popular family-run inn serves reliable Slow Food with leisurely service. There's lots of variety, from Venetian risotto to northern Italian game dishes, as well as fine wines. Booking advisable. Vaporetto: Ca' d'Oro. €€

GIUDECCA

RESTAURANTS

Altanella Calle delle Erbe, tel: 041-522 7780. Friendly trattoria favoured by Elton John, who has a home around the corner. Only fish dishes on offer, but also try the ice cream with grappa-soaked raisins. Lovely outdoor seating with sweeping views across the Giudecca Canal. No credit cards. Vaporetto: Palanca or Redentore. €€€

Harry's Dolci Fondamenta San Biagio, tel: 041-522 4844; www.cipriani. com. Come here for a waterside American brunch; it's Harry's without the hype, and with better views and prices. Try the Venetian risotto or, better still, come for cakes *(dolci)* outside mealtimes, or sip a signature Bellini in the bar. Vaporetto: Sant' Eufemia. €€€

BARS

Skyline Rooftop Bar Molino Stucky Hilton, Fondamenta San Biagio 810, www.skylinebarvenice.it. Sleek, award-winning venue both for the scenery – with wonderful views across the canal – and for the cocktails. Excellent spot to catch the sunset and begin your evening out with a (pricey) Bellini. Vaporetto: Palanca. €€€

THE OTHER ISLANDS

RESTAURANTS

Al Ponte del Diavolo Fondamenta Borgognoni 10, Isola di Torcello, www. osteriaalpontedeldiavolo.com. Set on Torcello, this inn is a charming rustic lunch venue. Vaporetto from Fondamenta Nuove to Torcello. **€€€**

Alla Maddalena Fondamenta di Santa Caterina 7C, Mazzorbo, tel: 041-730 151; www.trattoriamaddalena.com. Dine here for a superbly creative menu inspired by Veneto cuisine, Slow Food values and very local wines. That's if you're not tempted by **Venissa** next door (see below). Vaporetto: ferry 41/42 from Fondamenta Nuove to Mazzorbo, then cross the footbridge. **€€**

Venissa Fondamenta di Santa Caterina 3, Mazzordbo, www.venissa.it. An easy stroll across the bridge from Burano on the island of Mazzorbo, this Michel-starred restaurant looks onto a belltower at the centre of its own tiny vineyard with roots in the Middle Ages. Seasonal tasting menus revolve around the local riches caught and foraged from the lagoon and the Northern Adriatic. Boat transfer from Venice on offer. **€€€€**

Travel essentials

PRACTICAL INFORMATION

ACCESSIBLE TRAVEL

With its narrow alleys and stepped bridges, Venice is a challenge, especially if you are not travelling through a specialist tour operator or able to splash out on water taxis. **Accessible Italy** (www.accessibleitaly.com) is a good place to start your research. For transport tips, see **Venezia Unica** (www.veneziaunica.it) and find the 'Accessible Venice' section. Among other tips, you'll find a number of "barrier-free itineraries" for those with reduced mobility. All *vaporetto* (waterbus) stops are accessible to wheelchair users, who are entitled to discounted rates on tickets (which also cover one companion).

As for hotels, avoid the Santa Croce and San Polo areas, which are unsuitable, and ideally opt for a Grand Canal hotel near a ferry stop. Ramps along the Zattere make this delightful stroll more accessible. The **tourist office** supplies maps marking accessible areas, bridges with ramps for wheelchairs, and toilets for people with disabilities. Accessible attractions (note that no differentiation is made between full and partial access) include the Basilica San Marco, Palazzo Ducale, Ca' Rezzonico, and the churches of the Frari and La Salute.

ACCOMMODATION

Even if Venice has its fair share of palatial hotels, there is now great choice at the more modest end, from boutique retreats to chic guesthouses, eclectic B&Bs, intimate, family-owned *palazzi* and even barebones hostel beds. If you hanker after decadence and drama, choose a grand pile on the Grand Canal. If you yearn for a quiet life, chiming bells and secret gardens, slip into a family-owned *palazzo* in the backwaters of Cannaregio. Or, for a sense of stripped-back Venice before the interior decorators moved in, retreat to a bucolic inn on Burano, the lagoon's friendliest island. The lack of standardisation in Venetian hotels cuts both ways: each room is delightfully different but, on the other hand, even in a distinguished hotel, the rooms at the front may be glorious, but dingy garrets at the back.

Advance booking is essential during peak seasons (Carnival, Easter, May–June, Aug–Sep and Christmas). Hotels closest to San Marco tend to be pricier but search out midweek or seasonal deals online.

Opting for an apartment is a delightful way of experiencing the real city, even revelling in a Gothic *palazzo* complete with gondola dock. **Venetian Apartments** (www.veniceprestige.com) are market leaders, with a reliable range of fully-vetted apartments to suit couples, families or even celebratory house parties.

Venice's widest selection of hostels can be found on Giudecca, the biggest and best being **Generator Venice** (http://staygenerator.com). If staying outside the city, avoid soulless Mestre and opt for atmospheric Padua or Treviso, a 30-minute train ride from Venice.

I'd like a single/double room **Vorrei una camera singola/
matrimoniale**
with (without) bath/shower **con (senza) bagno/doccia**
What's the rate per night? **Qual è il prezzo per una notte?**

AIRPORTS

Venice Marco Polo airport (VCE; www.veniceairport.it) lies 13km (8 miles) north of the city. Regular public **buses** (ACTV; http://actv.avmspa.it) and airport buses (ATVO; www.atvo.it) run from the airport to the terminus at Piazzale Roma every quarter of an hour throughout most of the day; airport buses (ATVO; http://atvo.it) run at least twice per hour. Once at Piazzale Roma, board the No. 1 *vaporetto* (waterbus) for an all-stages ride along the Grand Canal; or take the No. 2 for the quickest route to San Marco. The Ponte Calatrava also connects you by foot to the main railway station.

Private water taxis are the speediest and most stylish way to arrive in Venice (30 minutes, from €120), whisking you from the airport right up to your hotel if it has a water entrance. Although not the cheapest option, it makes for a memorable and exciting experience.

Treviso (TSF; www.trevisoairport.it) is a small airport 32km (20 miles) north of Venice, used by charters and low-cost airlines such as Ryanair. It's also served by regular airport buses (ATVO; www.atvo.it).

APPS

The official AVM Venezia app (https://avm.avmspa.it) offers maps, timetables and ticketing for the waterbus network. For train travel to and from Venice's Santa Lucia station, arrive fully prepared with the handy Trenitalia app (www.trenitalia.com). During Venice's famous biennial art show, the La Biennale app (www.biennaleapp.com) offers routes and maps to lead you to the various pavilions.

Where's the boat/bus for…? **Dove si prende il vaporetto/
   l'autobus per…?**
I want a ticket to… **Desidero uno biglietto per…**
What time does the train/bus leave for the city centre? **A che
   ora parte il treno/pullman per il centro?**

BUDGETING FOR YOUR TRIP

The currency in Italy is the euro. For a rough guide as to how much things cost, the following is a list of average prices:

Drinks. Non-alcoholic drinks in bars and restaurants cost around €2.50–4; beer €3–5; glass of house wine €3–5.

Entertainment. A concert in a main church costs from €25; Fenice opera tickets from €100. Casino admission from €10.

Gondolas. From €80 for a 30-minute ride during the day (€120 for 50min); €100 for a 30-minute ride after 7pm (€150 for 50min).

Guided tours. For a walking tour, allow around €30.

Hotel. For bed and breakfast per night in high season, inclusive of tax: deluxe €400 and above; expensive, €280–400; moderate, €150–280; inexpensive, less than €150 (dorm beds from €40).

Lido beaches: from €10 (from the morning, including sunbed/parasol) but only around €3 after 2pm.

Meals. *Tramezzini* (small sandwiches) from €4; *cichetti* (hot and cold tapas at wine bars) from €3–4 per item; full meal for one at an inexpensive restaurant €25–30; at a moderate restaurant, including cover and service (excluding drinks) €40–50; pizza €8–15.

Museums and attractions. €3–20 (see page 135).

Public transport: €65 for 7 days, €45 for 3 days, €35 for 2 days, €25 for 1 day (24 hours). A ticket valid for 75 minutes costs €9.50.

CLIMATE

Venetian winters are cold, summers are hot, and the weather the rest of the year somewhere in between. The winds off the Adriatic and occasional flooding mean that Venice can be damp and chilly, although very atmospheric, between November and March. June, July and August can be stifling – air conditioning is pretty essential for a good night's rest at this time of year.

You might just be affected by high water *(acque alte)* in Venice in winter so be prepared. Tidal levels are calculated according to mean water levels at the Punta della Salute, facing St Mark's. When tides above 110cm are forecast, warning sirens wail, while duckboards are erected on key routes and by jetties; wellington boots are needed if tides are over 120cm (4ft), but the ferry *(vaporetto)* service remains operational. The good news is that although High Water follows the tidal cycle, six hours up and six hours down, very high water usually only lasts 3–4 hours before subsiding.

	J	F	M	A	M	J	J	A	S	O	N	D
Max												
°F	44	47	55	62	71	77	82	82	74	64	53	46
°C	7	8	12	17	22	25	28	28	23	18	12	8
Min												
°F	33	35	41	48	57	63	67	66	60	51	42	35
°C	1	1	5	9	14	17	19	19	16	11	6	2

CRIME AND SAFETY (see also Emergencies and Police)

Although Venice is incredibly safe, pickpockets are not uncommon, especially in the crowded areas around the Rialto and San Marco. Carry only what is absolutely necessary; leave the rest in the hotel safe. Make photo-copies of your passport and other vital documents to facilitate reporting any theft and obtaining replacements. Notify the police of any theft, so that they can give you a statement to file with your insurance claim.

I want to report a theft **Voglio denunciare un furto**

DRIVING

Venice is a **traffic-free zone**, and the closest you can get to the centre in a car is Piazzale Roma, where there are two large multi-storey car parks and good ferry services (http://avm.avmspa.it). There is also a huge multi-storey car park on the adjacent island of Tronchetto (www.interparkingi-talia.it), the terminal for the car ferry to the Lido, where driving is allowed. Tronchetto is linked to Venice (Piazzale Roma) via the monorail, called the People Mover. Although the outdoor car parks are guarded night and day, it's sensible not to leave anything of value in your car.

ELECTRICITY

The electrical current is 220V, AC, and sockets take two-pin round-pronged plugs. Bring an adaptor *(un adattatore)*, as required.

EMBASSIES AND CONSULATES

Most consulates have useful lists of English-speaking doctors, lawyers and interpreters, etc.

Australia: Via Borgogna 2, Milan, tel: 027-767 4200, https://italy.embassy.gov.au.

Canada: Via Verziere 11, Milan; consul.milan@international.gc.ca, www.international.gc.ca.

New Zealand: Via Clitunno 44, Rome; tel: 06-853 7501, www.mfat.govt.nz/en/embassies.

Republic of Ireland: Villa Spada, Via Giacomo Medici 1, Rome; tel: 06-585 2381, www.ireland.ie/en/italy/rome.

South Africa (honorary consulate): San Marco, 1386, Venice, tel: 041 24 06 870, www.lnx.sudafrica.it.

UK: Via XX Settembre 80/a, Rome, tel: 06-4220 0001, www.gov.uk/world/organisations/british-embassy-rome.

US: via Principe Amedeo 2/10, Milan; tel: 02-290 351, www.usembassy.gov.

EMERGENCIES

In case of an emergency, tel: Ambulance: **118**; Fire: **115**; Carabinieri: **112** (urgent police action); Police: **113**

GETTING THERE

By air. Companies flying from the UK include British Airways (www.britishairways.com), easyJet (www.easyjet.com), Ryanair (www.ryanair.com) and TUI Airways (www.tui.co.uk). Ryanair also run flights to Treviso airport (32km/20 miles from Venice) from several UK destinations, including London Southend. Aer Lingus (www.aerlingus.com) operate services from Dublin to Venice. From the US there are direct flights from New York (Delta Airlines, www.delta.com) and other gateways through Alitalia (www.alitalia.it).

By train. Venice's Stazione Venezia – Santa Lucia is well-connected to Turin, Milan, Florence and Rome, as well as to Paris, Vienna and London. Arriving by train can be a romantic experience, with the slowness offset by wonderful views through France and within sight of the Alps. Travel via Eurostar from London to Paris, then via Frecciarossa from Paris to Milan to connect to Venice! Alternatively, book a rail pass (International Rail, www.internationalrail.com), or – if prepared for a splurge – book a berth on the luxurious Venice Simplon-Orient-Express (www.belmond.com/trains).

GUIDES AND TOURS

St Mark's and the Doge's Palace: Free tours are given of the Basilica in summer, while **'Secret Routes'** (Itinerari Segreti; booking essential, http://palazzoducale.visitmuve.it) show you the ins and outs of life at the Palazzo Ducale, including a pass through the Chamber of the Secret Chancellery, the Chamber of Torture and the cells that once housed Casanova.

Brenta Canal cruise: a cruise to Padua aboard the 200-seater Burchiello (www.burchiello.it) motorboat traces how the Venetian nobility once lived in their summer villas.

Lagoon tours: Destination Venice (Campo San Luca, San Marco 4590, www.destination-venice.com) offer made-to-measure explorations of the lagoon and islands, along with individual guided walks, and Venetian-style rowing lessons. Thanks to the shifting tides and the shallowness of the lagoon, the islands preserve a pastoral way of life, one that is rarely visible to visitors who stay close to the shore. The lagoon is often dismissed as a desolate marsh but it is also a patchwork of sand banks, salt pans and mud flats, with sections cultivated as fish farms, market gardens and vineyards; much lagoon life survives, from kingfishers, cormorants and coots to grey herons and egrets. This is where Venetians retreat to go fishing, watch birds and sunbathe. At low tide, the shrimp fishermen leave their boats and seem to walk across water; families picnicking on remote sandbanks appear from nowhere and then disappear again with the tide.

Venice Kayak (www.venicekayak.com) offers refreshingly untouristy kayak tours around the city and lagoon, including seeing the sights from the water. Do day or night paddles from their base at Certosa Island, easily reached by *vaporetto* (from €110 for a 2hr 30min excursion).

HEALTH AND MEDICAL CARE

EU citizens: EU citizens are entitled to the same medical treatment as an Italian citizen. Visitors will need to have a European Health Insurance Card (EHIC, www.nhs.uk) before they go.

UK citizens: Italy and the UK have a reciprocal agreement regarding hospital treatment. UK citizens should obtain a UK-issued Global Health Insurance Card (GHIC, www.nhs.uk) before travelling. This entitles visitors to low-cost and sometimes free medical treatment. Full travel insurance, however, is still advised.

US citizens: If your private health insurance policy does not cover you while abroad, take out a short-term policy before leaving home.

Medical emergencies: Ask at your hotel or consulate if you need a doctor/dentist who speaks English. The **Guardia Medica** (tel: 041-529 4060) is a night call-out service. Many doctors at Ospedale SS. Giovanni e Paolo, Venice's only hospital, next to San Zanipolo, speak English; tel: 041-529 4111 (and ask for *'pronto soccorso'*, A&E/casualty).

Mosquitoes: A nuisance in Venice in summer, solved with a small plug-in machine.

Pharmacies: Italian *farmacie* open during shopping hours and in turn for night and holiday service; the address of the nearest open pharmacy is posted on all pharmacy doors.

> I need a doctor/dentist **Ho bisogno di un medico/dentista**
> I've a pain here **Ho un dolore qui**
> a stomach ache **il mal di stomaco**
> a fever **la febbre**

LANGUAGE

Most Venetian hotels and shops will have staff who speak some English, French or German. However, in bars and cafés away from Piazza San Marco, you'll almost certainly have the chance to practise your Italian. Locals will generally welcome attempts to use their language. When you enter a shop, restaurant or office, the greeting is always *buon giorno* (good morning) or *buona sera* (good afternoon/evening – used from around 1pm onwards). When enquiring, start with *per favore* (please), and for any service rendered say *grazie* (thanks), to which the reply is *prego* (don't mention it, you're welcome).

LGBTQ+ TRAVEL

While Venice is a welcoming destination for LGBTQ+ visitors, there is little in the way of a scene. The nearest clusters of specifically gay or lesbian bars are in Mestre and Padua, the latter also home to the nearest branch of Arcigay (http://arcigay.it), the national gay rights organisation. Another useful resource is www.gayfriendlyitaly.com.

MONEY

Italy's monetary unit is the euro (€), which is divided into 100 cents. Banknotes are available in denominations of 500, 200, 100, 50, 20, 10 and 5 euro. There are coins for 2 and 1 euro, and for 50, 20, 10, 5, 2 and 1 cents.

Currency exchange. *Bureau de change* offices *(cambi)* are usually open Monday to Friday, although hours do vary (Travelex offices at Piazza San Marco and the airport). Both *cambi* and banks charge a commission. Banks generally offer higher exchange rates and lower commissions. Passports are usually required when changing money.

ATMs and credit cards. Automatic currency-exchange machines *(bancomat)* are operated by most banks and can also be found in the centre of town. Most hotels, shops and restaurants take credit cards.

OPENING TIMES

Banks. Opening hours of banks in Italy tend to be more limited than in many other countries. Generally, hours are Mon–Fri 8.30am–1.30pm, 2.45–4pm.

Bars and restaurants. Some café-bars open for breakfast, but others do not open until around noon; the vast majority shut early, at around 10.30 or 11pm. Old-fashioned *bacari* (wine and tapas bars) in the Rialto area often close early (at around 9.30pm). Most restaurants close at least one day a week; some close for parts of August, January and February.

Churches. The majority of the 16 Chorus Churches are open Mon–Sat 10.30am–4.30pm. The Frari is also open Sun 1–6pm. Other churches are normally open Mon–Sat from around 8am until noon and from 3 or 4pm until 6 or 7pm. On Sunday, some are only open for morning services.

Museums and galleries. Most close on Monday, but are otherwise open at 9 or 10am until 6pm.

Shops. Business hours are Monday to Saturday, 9 or 10am until 1pm, and 3 or 4pm until 7pm. Some shops are open all day and even on Sundays, particularly in peak season.

PASSES

To save money (and, in certain instances, to skip the queue), choose from a number of prebooked, integrated passes covering transport and/or entry to a range of sites. The sites with the longest queues are St Mark's Basilica, the Doge's Palace and the Accademia. The attractions that must be prebooked are the Clock Tower and the Secret Itineraries tour of the Doge's Palace.

Chorus Pass (www.chorusvenezia.org): Full pass costs €12 and includes entry to 19 historical churches; a limited pass for €7 grants entry to any 3 of these.

Museum Pass (www.visitmuve.it): Grants access to 11 museums across Venice, including the Doge's Palace and Museo Correr.

Venezia Unica City Pass (www.veneziaunica.it): Customizable pass for public transport with ACTV plus museums and other city attractions.

Venice Pass (www.venicepass.eu): Includes public transport with ACTV and access to select museums, churches and galleries for two, three or five days.

POLICE

Although you rarely see them, Venice's police *(Polizia or Carabinieri)* function efficiently and are courteous. The emergency police telephone number is **112** or **113**; this will put you through to a switchboard and someone who speaks your language.

> Where's the nearest police station? **Dov'è il più vicino posto di polizia?**

PUBLIC HOLIDAYS

Banks, government offices and most shops and museums close on public holidays *(giorni festivi)*. When a major holiday falls on a Thursday or a Tuesday, Italians may make a *ponte* (bridge) to the weekend, meaning that Friday or Monday is taken, too.

The most important holidays are:

1 January **Capodanno** New Year

6 January **Epifania** (Epiphany)

25 April **Festa della Liberazione** Liberation Day

1 May **Festa del Lavoro** (Labour Day)

15 August **Ferragosto** (Assumption)

1 November **Ognissanti** (All Saints)

8 December **Immacolata Concezione** (Immaculate Conception)

25 December **Natale** (Christmas Day)

26 December **Santo Stefano** (Boxing Day)

Moveable Date **Pasquetta** (Easter Monday)

The **Festa della Salute** on 21 November and the **Redentore** on the third Sunday of July are special Venetian holidays, when many shops close.

RELIGION

Although predominantly Roman Catholic, Venice has congregations of all the major religions. If planning to enter Venice's churches or synagogues, dress to cover both shoulders and knees.

TELEPHONES

The country code for Italy is 39, and the area code for the city of Venice is 041. Note that you must dial the '041' prefix even when making local calls within the city of Venice. Smaller bars and businesses increasingly only have mobile numbers.

Mobile phones. EU mobile phones can be used in Italy, but check compatibility or buy an Italian SIM card, available from any mobile phone shop. Alternatively, you can purchase an eSIM online for a quick and easy way to connect to a local network. Mobile phone use in EU countries may be included in your plan at no extra cost but check with your local GSM dealer for information on roaming costs before visiting. Since Brexit, UK nationals are no longer guaranteed free roaming throughout the EU, but some networks may still offer this perk. As a non-EU visitor to Europe, make sure you check roaming rates with your provider before travelling.

International Calls. Dial 00, followed by the country code (Australia +61, Ireland +353, New Zealand +64, South Africa +27, UK +44, US and Canada +1), then the area code (often minus the initial zero) and finally the individual number.

TIME

Italy is one hour ahead of Greenwich Mean Time (GMT). From the last Sunday in March to the last Sunday in October, clocks are put forward an hour.

TIPPING

A service charge of 10 or 12 percent is often added to restaurant bills, so it is not necessary to tip much – perhaps just round the bill up. However, it is normal to tip bellboys, porters, tour guides and elderly gondoliers who help you into and out of your boat at the landing stations.

TOILETS

There are public toilets *(toilette, gabinetti)* usually with a charge, at the airport and railway station. Most people use the facilities in bars but only if you order a drink. *Signori* means men; *signore* means women.

> Where are the toilets? **Dove sono i gabinetti?**

TOURIST INFORMATION

The most central tourist office (APT) is at the southwestern corner of Piazza San Marco (Piazza San Marco 71/f; www.veneziaunica.it), opposite the Museo Correr. As well as maps and brochures, staff can book tours and events. Additional branches are found at Marco Polo airport and Piazzale Roma.

TRANSPORT

Vaporetti (water buses). These workhorses will take you to within a short walk of anywhere you want to visit. Find updated maps, routes and timetables at https://actv.avmspa.it. The main waterbus services are: **No. 1**, which stops at every landing stage along the Grand Canal; **No. 2**, provides a faster service down the Grand Canal as part of its circular San Marco, Giudecca Canal, Piazzale Roma route (and the Lido). **Nos 4.1** (anticlockwise) and **4.2** (clockwise) describe Venice in a circular route, calling at San Zaccaria, Il Redentore (Palladio's masterpiece), Piazzale Roma, Ferrovia (the railway station), Fondamenta Nuove, San Michele, Murano and Sant'Elena. Vaporetti **5.1** and **5.2** also provide long, scenic, circular tours around the periphery, as well as stopping at Murano; in summer they go on to the Lido (change at Fondamenta Nuove to do the whole route). Note that the circular routes travel up the Cannaregio canal, stopping at Guglie, and then skirting the northern shores of Venice, including Fondamenta Nuove and the Madonna dell'Orto (Tintoretto's church), the shipyards (Bacini stop), San Pietro di Castello and, eventually, the Lido. **No. 6** provides a fast route between Piazzale Roma and the Lido, going via the Zattere (Giudecca Canal). Hop on the lagoon lines (Nos 11, 12, 13, 14, 15, 20 and 22) to get to the outer islands, including Murano and Burano. **Line 9** connects Burano with Torcello.

When's the next *vaporetto* for…? **A che ore parte il prossimo vaporetto per…?**

What's the fare to…? **Quanto costa il biglietto per…?**

I want a ticket to… **Vorrei un biglietto per…**

Gondolas. The official daytime rate is €80 for 30 minutes (up to six people), then €40–50 for each subsequent 20 minutes. The evening rate (from 7pm) is €100.

Water taxis (*motoscafi*). These are for a door-to-door service that comes with a high cost.

Traghetti. The *traghetto* (gondola ferry, locals 70 cents, tourists €2) operates at key points across the Grand Canal. It is customary (but not obligatory) to stand while crossing.

Walking. It is often quicker (and cheaper) to walk so enjoy getting lost on foot: official addresses are confusing so always ask for the name of the nearest church or square (*campo*).

VISA AND ENTRY REQUIREMENTS

Visa-free entry. For citizens of the United Kingdom, US, Australia, Canada and New Zealand, among other countries (full list at www.esteri.it), a valid passport is all that is needed to enter Italy for stays of up to 90 days within an 180-day period.

Visas. For stays of more than 90 days, a visa *(permesso di soggiorno)* or residence permit is required. Regulations change from time to time, so check with the Italian Embassy (www.esteri.it) or in your home country before you travel.

Customs. Free exchange of non-duty-free goods for personal use is allowed between countries within the European Union (EU). Refer to your home country's regulating organisation for a current list of import restrictions.

Currency restrictions. A customs declaration is required to bring €10,000 cash (or equivalent in currency) into or out of the country.

Index

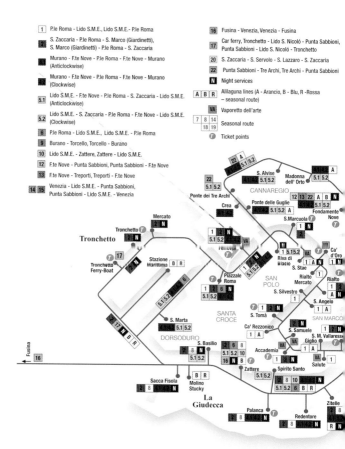

1 P.le Roma - Lido S.M.E., Lido S.M.E. - P.le Roma	**16** Fusina - Venezia, Venezia - Fusina
2 S. Zaccaria - P.le Roma - S. Marco (Giardinetti), S. Marco (Giardinetti) - P.le Roma - S. Zaccaria	**17** Car ferry, Tronchetto - Lido S. Nicoló - Punta Sabbioni, Punta Sabbioni - Lido S. Nicoló - Tronchetto
3 Murano - F.te Nove - P.le Roma - F.te Nove - Murano (Anticlockwise)	**20** S. Zaccaria - S. Servolo - S. Lazzaro - S. Zaccaria
4 Murano - F.te Nove - P.le Roma - F.te Nove - Murano (Clockwise)	**22** Punta Sabbioni - Tre Archi, Tre Archi - Punta Sabbioni
5.1 Lido S.M.E. - F.te Nove - P.le Roma - S. Zaccaria - Lido S.M.E. (Anticlockwise)	**N** Night services
5.2 Lido S.M.E. - S. Zaccaria - P.le Roma - F.te Nove - Lido S.M.E. (Clockwise)	**A B R** Alilaguna lines (A - Arancio, B - Blu, R -Rossa) – seasonal lines
6 P.le Roma - Lido S.M.E., Lido S.M.E. - P.le Roma	**VA** Vaporetto dell'arte
9 Burano - Torcello, Torcello - Burano	**7 8 14 18 19** Seasonal route
10 Lido S.M.E. - Zattere, Zattere - Lido S.M.E.	Ticket points
12 F.te Nove - Punta Sabbioni, Punta Sabbioni - F.te Nove	
13 F.te Nove - Treporti, Treporti - F.te Nove	
14 15 Venezia - Lido S.M.E. - Punta Sabbioni, Punta Sabbioni - Lido S.M.E. - Venezia	

Venice Vaporetti Network

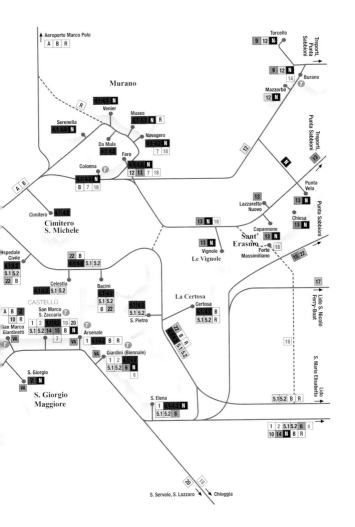

THE **MINI** ROUGH GUIDE TO
VENICE

First edition 2025

Editor: Lizzie Horrocks
Updater: Anthon Jackson
Author: Rob Ullian
Picture Editor: Piotr Kala
Picture Manager: Tom Smyth
Cartography Update: Katie Bennett
Layout: Grzegorz Madejak
Production Operations Manager: Katie Bennett
Publishing Technology Manager: Rebeka Davies
Head of Publishing: Sarah Clark
Photography Credits: All images **Shutterstock** except: Anna Mockford and Nick Bonetti/Apa Publications 79; Dreamstime 7, 19; Glyn Genin/Apa Publications 10BL, 75; Hilton Hotels & Resorts 12BR; iStock 10TL, 10CR, 10BR, 11T, 11CT, 11CB, 12TL, 12BL, 36, 48, 51, 56, 62, 70, 83, 101; Public domain 21, 22, 24; Starwood Hotels & Resorts 109
Cover Credits: Houses on Burano **Shutterstock**

About the updater

Anthon Jackson is a Utah-born, Denmark-based writer and photographer. He has contributed to more than 25 travel books for Rough Guides and other series. Follow Anthon on Instagram @anthonjackson, on X @janthonjackson, and visit his website, anthonjackson.com.

Distribution

UK, Ireland and Europe: Apa Publications (UK) Ltd; sales@roughguides.com
United States and Canada: Ingram Publisher Services; ips@ingramcontent.com
Australia and New Zealand: Booktopia; retailer@booktopia.com.au

Worldwide: Apa Publications (UK) Ltd; sales@roughguides.com

Special Sales, Content Licensing and CoPublishing

Rough Guides can be purchased in bulk quantities at discounted prices. We can create special editions, personalised jackets and corporate imprints tailored to your needs. sales@roughguides.com; http://roughguides.com

Contact us

Every effort has been made to provide accurate information in this publication, but changes are inevitable. The publisher cannot be held responsible for any resulting loss, inconvenience or injury sustained by any traveller as a result of information or advice contained in the guide. We would appreciate it if readers would call our attention to any errors or outdated information, or if you feel we've left something out. Please send your comments with the subject line "Rough Guide Mini Venice Update" to mail@uk.roughguides.com.